STO

ACPL IT █████████████████
SO-AUH-635
DISCARDED

338.947/ Y71

YUGOSLAVIA IN THE AGE OF
DEMOCRACY

**DO NOT REMOVE
CARDS FROM POCKET**

**ALLEN COUNTY PUBLIC LIBRARY
FORT WAYNE, INDIANA 46802**

You may return this book to any agency, branch,

or bookmobile of the Allen County Public Library.   DEMCO

YUGOSLAVIA
IN THE
AGE OF DEMOCRACY

YUGOSLAVIA IN THE AGE OF DEMOCRACY

Essays on Economic and Political Reform

Edited by
George Macesich

with the assistance of Rikard Lang,
Ljubisav Markovic, and Dragomir Vojnic

Foreword by Bernard F. Sliger

Westport, Connecticut
London

Allen County Public Library
900 Webster Street
PO Box 2270
Fort Wayne, IN 46801-2270

Library of Congress Cataloging-in-Publication Data

Yugoslavia in the age of democracy : essays on economic and political
reform / edited by George Macesich ; with the assistance of Rikard
Lang, Ljubisav Markovic, and Dragomir Vojnic ; foreword by Bernard
F. Sliger
    p. cm.
  Includes bibliographical references and index.
  ISBN 0-275-94175-2 (alk. paper)
    1. Yugoslavia—Economic conditions—1945- 2. Yugoslavia—Economic
policy—1945- 3. Yugoslavia—Politics and government—1945-
I. Macesich, George.
  HC407.Y822 1992
  338.9497—dc20   91-34495

British Library Cataloguing in Publication Data is available.

Copyright © 1992 by George Macesich

All rights reserved. No portion of this book may be
reproduced, by any process or technique, without the
express written consent of the publisher.

Library of Congress Catalog Card Number: 91-34495
ISBN: 0-275-94175-2

First published in 1992

Praeger Publishers, 88 Post Road West, Westport, CT 06881
An imprint of Greenwood Publishing Group, Inc.

Printed in the United States of America

The paper used in this book complies with the
Permanent Paper Standard issued by the National
Information Standards Organization (Z39.48-1984).

10 9 8 7 6 5 4 3 2 1

DEDICATION

Branimir M. Jankovic, Ph.D.
Professor of International Law and Diplomacy
1920-1990

Branimir M. Jankovic

November 13, 1920 -- September 26, 1990

Branimir M. Jankovic was professor of international law and diplomacy at the University of Belgrade (1948-90) and a visiting professor and research scholar in international/contemporary law for almost thirty years at the Center for Yugoslav-American Studies, Research, and Exchanges at the Florida State University. He was a member of the Center's Joint Advisory Council.

He received his Ph.D. from the Faculty of Law, University of Belgrade (1953), and studied at the Academy of International Law-The Hague (1951-53), at Harvard University (1960), and at the University of California at Berkeley (1961) under Ford Foundation fellowships. He was the recipient of numerous honors and university medals for his lectures in European universities. His numerous publications have appeared in English, German, French, and Serbo-Croat.

His legal and teaching career ranged from participation in international seminars and symposiums in political science/science technology to membership in the Yugoslav delegation to the United Nations. He later served the United Nations as a legal expert covering human rights in Africa and Asia and protection of minorities, and served on the staff of UNESCO.

Contents

Tables

Foreword

This work is the latest publication resulting from one of the most stable and productive international exchange programs in the academic world. I believe you will find it to be a piece of sound scholarship. I also hope you will see it as a symbol of the understanding and appreciation which rewards the hard work of those who labor to overcome barriers of language, culture, politics, ideology, and distance in their pursuit of knowledge.

The Florida State University/Yugoslavia Exchange Program began in 1961. At first it was only an exchange of scholars in economics between FSU and the University of Belgrade. That simple beginning was remarkable, however, considering the climate of the times. (The Berlin Wall was built in 1961.) Professor George Macesich of FSU and Professor Branimir Jankovic of Belgrade deserve full credit for the origination of the program. Their determination not only sustained the exchange in economics but strengthened it and eventually led to the inclusion of other universities and other fields of study. Numerous other individuals provided invaluable assistance that made ultimate success possible. Foremost among them were professors Marshall R. Colberg, Dragomir Vojnic, Ljubisav Markovic, Ljubisa S. Adamovic, Stojan Bulat, Dimitrije Dimitrijevic, and Rikard Lang.

Many visitors to our campus are surprised to find a Yugoslav Center. Florida has no extraordinary population of Yugoslav descent; we share no borders and serve no common master; and Serbo-Croatian is hardly the vernacular of the Panhandle. "Why," I am often asked, "did you develop a joint program with universities in Yugoslavia?"

The first reason, of course, is the presence of Professor Macesich. He is of Yugoslav descent; he is schooled in international economics; he is diligent; and he is persuasive. The second reason is our interest in the peoples of Yugoslavia and the republics of the former Yugoslav federation. Macesich opened a window for us and forced some of us to look. After that, the beauty and complexity of Yugoslavia became a magnet for our minds. The language, art, economics, history, political science, public policy, law, natural science, trade, and numerous other aspects of life in Yugoslavia were treasure houses of new knowledge for us Floridians.

We found our interest reciprocated, and we began to exchange ideas as well as people. I believe that participants from both countries have made discoveries about themselves as well as about their colleagues. This, I expect, is the alpha and the omega of international exchange in the academy.

Since 1961, over 1,000 persons have participated in the Florida-Yugoslavia exchange. They have lectured and listened, studied and taught, published, and read. Knowledge in many fields has increased and, perhaps most important of all, a vast resource of goodwill and genuine understanding has been firmly established.

Today, the Yugoslav Center on our campus is a busy and productive place, to which leaders of government, industry, and education frequently turn for information and understanding about two great peoples. I believe this will be the case for decades to come.

Bernard F. Sliger, Former President
Professor of Economics
Florida State University

YUGOSLAVIA
IN THE
AGE OF DEMOCRACY

Introduction

This book commemorates the thirtieth anniversary of the Center for Yugoslav-American Studies, Research, and Exchanges at the Florida State University, which also makes it the thirtieth anniversary of the Center's programs in comparative policy studies. The book is an addition to a growing list of studies undertaken by the Center. These include such recent studies as George Macesich, Rikard Lang, and Dragomir Vojnic, eds., Essays on the Political Economy of Yugoslavia (1982); Dimitrije Dimitrijevic and George Macesich, Money and Finance in Yugoslavia: A Comparative Analysis (1984); Dan Voich, Jr., and Mijat Damjanovic, eds, Essays on Comparative Managerial Practices in the U. S. and Yugoslavia (1985); T. Misha Sarkovic, Direct Foreign Investment in Yugoslavia: A Microeconomic Model (1986); Vlasta Andrlic and Ljiljana Jovkovic, eds., Dictionary of Yugoslav Political and Economic Terminology (English/Serbo-Croatian) (1985); George Macesich, Rikard Lang, and Dragomir Vojnic, eds., Yugoslav Economic Model (1989); Dimitrije Dimitrijevic and George Macesich, Money Supply Process: A Comparative Analysis (1990); and George Macesich, Reform and Market Democracy (1991).

This present book deals with the economic and political reforms in Yugoslavia. Countries seeking democratic reforms should study Yugoslavia's experience for guidance on what to do and what not to do. Yugoslavia is a country overburdened with more than $17 billion in foreign debt and an estimated $10 billion in internal debt. It suffers from crippling inflation and inefficient industry. It has been hurt by an oversized bureaucracy, a work force without incentives, poor planning, poor politics, and other problems. And it must overcome ancient nationalistic rivalries among its republics before it can pull out of its vast economic, political, and social problems. Can Yugoslavia do it? If goodwill prevails among all of the participants in the process, there is room for optimism.

In the course of its ongoing economic and political reforms, Yugoslavia must develop a true pluralistic democracy and a free, market-oriented society, with private property and civil rights. It must transcend narrow nationalism and allow everyone freedom to develop. At the same time, its new democratic parties must embrace the entire nation and not just individual republics or single nationalities.

Experience with the processes of reform in Yugoslavia and elsewhere[1] indicates that quality people are required to carry out quality reforms. To be sure, quality politicians are in short supply the world over. However, although good government in democratic societies is difficult, it is not impossible. When the structures and incentives are right, it is possible to transform the performance of many dynamic workers who were held back by the old system. At the same time, it is important to replace those people who cannot or will not adapt to the new environment.

When the objectives of reform are clearly defined, it is important to implement the reforms with speed. If the implementation is hesitant, various interest groups will likely sabotage the reforms. The economy operates as an organic whole, not as an unrelated collection of bits and pieces. Costs, moreover, appear immediately while the benefits may take time to be realized. It is uncertainty, not speed, that endangers structural reform programs, as Yugoslavia's experience underscores.

The momentum must be maintained until the entire program is completed. Opponents of reform are not likely to give up their privileges and protection easily. Reformers and their government must stay ahead, to lead the public debate.

Removing privileges evenly across the board diminishes the opposition of vested interest groups while enabling all factions a more constructive role in a reformed society. To keep public confidence in the reform venture and to minimize the costs of the undertaking, it is important to maintain credibility. Thus, it is essential that policy be consistent and communications open and effective. The public must be kept fully informed and consider itself an active participant in the reform processes.

Yugoslav experience over several decades of effort at reform is important here. An underlying difficulty with the country's earlier reforms was that they lacked a national consensus of objectives. For the most part, they did not seriously address the crucial issues of private property rights, free and open markets, a proper monetary and financial organization to serve a modern market economy, and the important issue of multiparty politics. Thereby, it missed an opportunity to promote the separation of the state and bureaucratic apparatus from political control by a single party.

Instead, the Yugoslavs sought reform through socialist decentralized worker self-management. The shortcomings of such an arrangement were obvious very early. I have discussed these elsewhere, as have other writers.[2] Consequently, there is little point in discussing them here except to underscore that while workers had the right to control and manage their respective firms, and while they had direct personal interest in the income produced, they did not own their firms. Since they could not sell their firms, they had little interest in the firm's market value. Worker interest in the firms' income also left something to be desired, because if they left the firm, they could sell their interests in the firm's future profits and income. Such an arrangement assures that workers will opt for an increase in current income at the expense of new investment and preservation of assets. Moreover, the problems are compounded by a lack of labor mobility and the disincentive for recruitment of new workers that such an arrangement assures.

To keep these firms going, to keep the worker-managers from decapitalizing their firms and to force additional workers upon them, the bureaucracy in the country expanded at all levels, assuring that vested interests would serve to undercut and side-track serious economic and political reform. At the same time, the socialist worker-managed firms were assured ready access to credit and borrowing and thus protected from bankruptcy. This arrangement removed constraints from the workers, increasing their salaries as well as providing incentives to increase efficiency.

The net result has been to impart into the Yugoslav economy a highly inflationary bias. The socialist worker-managers, with direct access to banks, and the National Bank's inability to impose restraint assured trouble for the Yugoslav experiment. The limitations and the problems in the country's monetary and financial organization have been discussed at length elsewhere.[3]

Various suggestions for quickly privatizing the Yugoslav firms have been made. One particularly important approach has been suggested by Marshall R. Colberg, and a similar one by Milton Friedman. Essentially both would turn over equity shares to the worker-managers, and thus provide these workers with private property rights in the firm. The recently established stock exchange would be empowered to trade in these equities.[4]

To enact the right policies and remain in power, a political leadership needs both political legitimacy and a supporting constituency. In the past, the Yugoslav leadership has implemented reforms piecemeal, more or less soldering various market reforms into the socialist worker-management model. This has created inflation, unemployment, and little gain. The Yugoslav model needs to be transformed into a real market economy. Otherwise, the experiment with socialist worker-management will become an obstacle to reform and a milepost on the road to economic disaster and political chaos.

Equally important to the reform process is the ongoing debate, which has strong nationalist and ethnic overtones, over the structure of Yugoslavia and whether it will continue with a federal or a confederate or indeed even a looser organization of the several republics. It is useful to briefly consider the economic implications of nationalism as they would likely apply to Yugoslavia and its several republics. For this purpose, I draw on the work of Harry G. Johnson, Albert Breton, Anthony Downs, Gary S. Becker, James M. Buchanan, Gordon Tullock, and my own earlier work on economic nationalism.[5]

Downs argues that political parties attempt to maximize the gains from political office by catering to the tastes and preferences of voters. In a multiparty democratic society, political parties remain in office only by satisfying these tastes and preferences with various types and amounts of government programs. In effect, political power is exchanged for desired policies in a transaction between party and electorate.

The critical element in Downs's hypothesis is the cost of acquiring information. He uses this cost to explain (1) reliance on persuasion in arriving at political decisions, (2) the inequality of political influence, (3) the role of ideology, (4) electoral apathy, and (5) the bias in democratic government toward serving producer rather than consumer interests.

Breton's analysis of economic nationalism identifies nationality with ownership by nationals of various types of property. He considers nationality to be a type of collective consumption capital, yielding an income of utility that can be invested in by spending public funds for the acquisition of such capital. From these assumptions he derives a number of testable propositions about nationalism.

These propositions about nationalism imply, among other things, that nationalist policy is primarily concerned with redistributing rather than increasing income. The redistribution, moreover, is from the working class to the middle class. As a result, when the working class is poor there will be a tendency to resort to confiscation rather than purchase. Since manufacturing jobs and ownership are preferred by the middle class, nationalism will tend to favor investment in national manufacturing. Given its collective nature, nationalism will strike a particularly responsive chord in socialists. Furthermore, the blossoming and appeal of nationalism will be closely associated with the rise of new middle classes whose members have difficulty in finding suitable career opportunities.

Johnson develops and extends Downs' cost of information on voter preferences and broadens Downs' concept of established democracies to include emerging countries. Thus, in the exchange between political parties and their electorate, the main obstacle to efficiency is ignorance on both sides about the prospective gains from the policies offered and about the cost of acquiring the information necessary to make the exchange efficient. This obstacle forces the political party to depend on pressure groups, lobbyists, and the communications media for its information about voter preferences. One consequence of this dependence is to give political parties a strong incentive to gain control over the communications media as a means of establishing control over the country. Indeed, the recent push by emerging countries for a "new information order" is consistent with Johnson's hypothesis.

The average voter is motivated by rational self-interest not to acquire much information about the policies of political parties and the consequences of these policies for his own economic welfare. Well

5

informed or not, he will have negligible influence on which party is elected. Given this motive for remaining ignorant, ideology steps in to play a key role in political affairs. Ideology simplifies a political party's problems in communicating with its electorate by summarizing its policies in symbolism or slogans. Thus the voter's problem is also simplified, since he can vote by ideology instead of investing his time in evaluating each party's record and promises on a whole range of particular policy issues. As a result, parties tend to compete through ideologies.

In established democracies, the type of party system that emerges will depend on a variety of features, including the distribution among voters of ideological preferences, the type of election system (proportional representation or plurality), and the geographical distribution of voter preferences. Proportionality tends to foster a multiplicity of ideologically differentiated parties, while plurality elections tend to promote a two-party system, except where ideological differences are associated with geographical region. In a multiparty system, because of the necessity of forming coalitions to obtain power, actual policy tends to present a compromise among ideologies. In a two-party system, party ideologies are determined by the distribution of voter preferences. Thus, if the distribution of voter preference is unimodal, there will be a grouping around a central ideological position and the party ideologies of the two parties do not differ significantly. On the other hand, if voter preferences are multimodal, then voter preferences that group around two or more ideological positions will become very important. If a party departs too significantly from its ideological position, it may alienate its constituents, who will tend not to vote. Worse, if party ideologies are significantly differentiated, the country itself will tend to be politically unstable and ripe for disintegration.

Matters are somewhat different if democracy is not well established. The incentive then is for a political party to attempt to create a comprehensive and preclusive ideology to enable it to enjoy exclusive control of the government. Emerging countries, observes Johnson, are particularly susceptible on this score. In emerging countries, a change in government is also likely to impose significant costs on those who have to wait for political office, costs that are not imposed on those who hold power and political office permanently.

To be sure, even in developed democracies, the change of office by political parties tends to be wasteful. However, the socioeconomic and political systems in such countries tend to reabsorb ousted political officeholders without imposing great private losses on them. The ability of these socioeconomic and political systems not to impose undue losses on political losers, as well as their acceptance of the rules of the game of democracy and its principles, are important in cultivating workable democracies.

It is the nationalistic feeling that provides a foundation for the establishment of a preclusive ideology as a prerequisite for a single-party government. Johnson calls attention to the connection between the stridency of nationalism in emerging countries and their propensity to establish a one-party government. However, even where the two-party system is maintained, the competition in ideology would tend to make both parties stress nationalism and nationalist policies if there were widespread nationalist sentiment among the electorate. Johnson succinctly observes that only if there is a sharp division of voter preferences, with some voters envisaging serious disadvantages, will there be significant political division on the issues and the likelihood of threat to the political stability.

Downs, moreover, underscores that the working of political democracy will display a certain asymmetry between producer and consumer interests. The concentration will be on producer interests, often at the expense of those of the consumer. Johnson extends this observation to nationalism and nationalist policies. Since producer costs can be spread thinly over a mass of consumers, nationalist policies win political support more readily by promoting producer interests, even though the net benefits, taking consumers and producers together, tend to be negative.

Our theoretical framework thus far outlines the working of political democracy and party government, integrating nationalism in emerging countries into the framework. We can draw on Becker's work on racial discrimination and Johnson's interpretation to consider nationalism as a cultivated preference and call it a "taste for nationalism." This is identical with Becker's concept of "taste for discrimination." That is, people who discriminate actually are willing to give up pecuniary returns for doing so in return for the nonpecuniary, or psychic, income derived from

7

avoiding the group discriminated against. In Becker's study the group discriminated against was Negroes in the United States. Johnson substitutes "taste for nationalism" for Becker's "taste for discrimination." Accordingly, the taste for nationalism attaches utility to certain jobs or certain property owned by members of the national group that is doing the discriminating; even though pecuniary returns are foregone as a result of exercising such tastes.

The types of property and jobs to which such utility is attached are obviously the prestige jobs and the socially significant property. These include, for example, literary and cultural activities, political and economic activities, properties with high prestige, and high incomes. The nationalist utility attached to the various properties, jobs, and cultural or other activities is derived internally, from an emerging country's colonial era, or externally, by observations about what takes place in more developed countries.

Nationalism is a collective consumption good, or public good, consumption of which by one individual does not exclude its consumption by others. The problem is one of determining the optimum amount of nationalism to supply. The specific benefits of nationalism obviously go to those select nationals who acquire those offices or property rights in which nationalism invests. These would include bureaucratic, elite, and producer interests. Thanks to the desire of cultural, linguistic, and communication interests to cultivate monopoly power, they are natural beneficiaries of a policy of economic nationalism. All of these interests are vulnerable to foreign competition.

Since everyone in the national state must consume the same quantity and quality of the public "nationalism" good, even though preferences and tax payments for the good may vary, it is not surprising that there is considerable controversy on the output and resource input of public goods by the nation-state. Some consumers want more and some less. Few will agree on what is the optimal quantity.

Collective decisions in political markets are complex. People can communicate their desire for public goods through voting behavior. Still, what a consumer-voter desires in a political market may be significantly different from what he or she ultimately receives. The correlation between a voter's choice and the expected outcome may be very weak. Efficient political decisions tend to affect

8

everyone in the community, unlike decisions in a private market, which affect primarily the consumer and supplier of a given product or service.

Moreover, if the demand for nationalism as a "club good" by the elite and bureaucracy is added to the demand by the general population for nationalism as a public good, it is likely that there will be an overproduction of nationalism. This will tend to allocate too many resources to the creation and preservation of the nation-state, including the creation and preservation of a formidable bureaucracy and military.

It is thus imperative that the bureaucracy and elite be discouraged and constrained from the use of nationalism to maximize their return and advantages. One way is to structure the incentive system to prevent, or at best limit, abuse of their authority. I recommend a system of well defined guides within lawful policy systems. In effect, I argue for a system of rules that constrains the bureaucracies and elites from discretionary exercise of power. The more closely constrained their actions are by rules or performance criteria, the less their power and prestige and the less their interests will coalesce with an excess production of nationalism.

As a public good, economic nationalism in particular appeals to the elite and bureaucracy and perhaps specific producer interests, whereas the costs are spread out over the mass of consumers. The political support for nationalist economic policies is obtained on the basis of the gains this group promises to its constituents, even if the total net benefits to all concerned tend to be negative.

As a policy, economic nationalism is encumbered by at least three biases:

1. It concentrates on industrialization, usually at the expense of agriculture. The objective here is to achieve a modern-looking nation-state as quickly as possible. The bias for industrialization is usually also specific in terms of the types of industries to encourage. The selection is more on the criterion of what leading developed nations possess than on comparative advantage and economic logic. The establishment of a steel industry, an automobile industry, and a national airline are but the more obvious cases in point.

2. There is a preference for economic planning, a feeling that the controls associated with

planning enable a country to more quickly mobilize available resources to achieve the other desired goals of nationalism. There is, in general, the perception that the processes of economic development are speeded up as a result of planning. Finally, the elite and bureaucracy see in planning a direct means of exercising and enhancing their power and prestige.

3. There is indiscriminate hostility to large multinational or transnational corporations. They are viewed as agents of the colonialism and imperialism of the advanced countries in which they happen to have their headquarters, and thus they are seen to pose a threat to the national sovereignty and independence of emerging countries. In effect such a corporation is viewed simply as an arm of the economic and political power of its parent country. Since these corporations are usually independent entities, they are viewed suspiciously both by host and parent countries. The parent countries complain that the corporations ought to invest and produce more at home rather than send employment opportunities abroad and create balance-of-payments problems for the country.

It may be that the nonpecuniary gains by the mass of the population from the collective-consumption aspects of nationalism offset the losses in primary income imposed on them by policies of economic nationalism, so that nationalistic policies do result in maximizing total satisfaction. It may also be that nationalistic policies are, in effect, the simplest and cheapest means of raising real income in some emerging countries. However, economic nationalism may so block economic growth that it becomes necessary to resort to even more extreme nationalistic sentiment and policy, as the only means available to maintain the illusion of economic development.

The economic significance of nationalism is thus a tendency to cultivate and extend property rights and jobs to nationals so as to satisfy their taste for nationalism. Confiscation and nationalization are ways to carry out such a policy. These measures affect property and usually affect jobs. Investment is another route whereby public funds are used to purchase property and create jobs and activities on behalf of nationals. It would also include imposing tariffs and in general protecting the activities of nationals, who would thereby receive higher prices, which in effect would be taxes imposed on the general consumer.

By reducing the efficiency of the country's economy, these by-products of economic nationalism also reduce its real income. Disappointment with the economy's performance on this score increasingly pushes the government into regulating prices and wages, to assure desired outcomes. This typically leads to price and wage controls. Since the controls inevitably fail, the system is then driven into collective participatory planning, where wages and prices are determined. This may, in fact, be desired by some people. Nevertheless, under such an arrangement there is little chance that the market system will be allowed to play its efficient role.

If Yugoslavia is headed toward a looser union, this does not necessarily mean the end of its identity. There are alternatives, and disintegration can be averted.

I have discussed one such alternative elsewhere. This alternative is to tie together into a common market the economically, politically, ethnically, and socially diverse countries or societies of Yugoslavia by means of flexible exchange rates.[6] Each republic would enjoy economic and political freedom to pursue independent policies. Mistakes and successes in their respective internal policies, including those concerning property rights and free markets, would be quickly reflected in the exchange rates between the republics. None would be able to inflict these mistakes on the others. A minimal central authority, the jurisdiction of which would include monetary and fiscal areas and perhaps defense and foreign affairs, would be given only such powers as the republics delegated to it. The precise details could be readily worked out.

Which direction suits Yugoslavia? Her friends hope that it is toward private property, free and open markets, a multiparty system, and human and civil rights that transcend narrow nationalism and ethnic and religious bigotry. These would be better for freedom and peace and better for the standard of living for all Yugoslavs. The basic choices are for Yugoslavs to make.

The essays in this volume, which focus on the critical issues that now confront the country in its continuing search for reform, stability, and unity, were written prior to recognition of the independence of Slovenia, Croatia, and Bosnia-Herzegovina by countries of the European community, the United

States, and others. The newly independent countries of the former Yugoslav federation will continue to occupy the same geographic and economic space. Their future economic and sociopolitical relations will provide many other opportunities for association. These essays provide valuable insight into the policies that may evolve from these relations and are more than of just historical interest.

I am grateful to many colleagues for useful comments and suggestions. I would also like to express appreciation for editorial assistance to Esther C. S. Glenn and for the efficient typing services of Beverly McNeil.

NOTES

1. Roger Douglas, "The Politics of Successful Structural Reforms," <u>Wall Street Journal</u>, January 17, 1990.

2. Chapter 6, "Workers' Management," and Chapter 7, "The Firm," in George Macesich, <u>Yugoslavia: Theory and Practice of Development Planning</u> (Charlottesville: University Press of Virginia, 1964); George Macesich, Rikard Lang, and Dragomir Vojnic, eds., <u>Essays on the Political Economy of Yugoslavia</u> (Zagreb: Informator, 1982); George Macesich, ed., with Rikard Lang and Dragomir Vojnic, <u>Essays on the Yugoslav Economic Model</u> (New York: Praeger, 1989).

3. Dimitrije Dimitrijevic and George Macesich, <u>Money and Finance in Contemporary Yugoslavia</u> (New York: Praeger 1973); and Dimitrije Dimitrijevic and George Macesich, <u>Money and Finance in Yugoslavia: A Comparative Analysis</u> (New York: Praeger, 1984).

4. Marshall R. Colberg, "Property Rights and Motivation: United States and Yugoslavia," <u>Proceedings and Reports</u>, Center for Yugoslav-American Studies, Research, and Exchanges, Florida State University, vols. 12-13 (1978-1979), pp. 52-58; Milton Friedman as interviewed by Drago Baum, <u>Privredni Vjesnik</u>, February 15, 1990.

5. Harry G. Johnson, ed., <u>Economic Nationalism in Old and New States</u> (Chicago: University of Chicago Press, 1967); Albert Breton, "The Economics of Nationalism," <u>Journal of Political Economy</u> 72 (1964): 376-86; Anthony Downs, <u>An Economic Theory of Democracy</u> (New York: Harper, 1957); Gary S. Becker, <u>The Economics of Discrimination</u> (Chicago: University of Chicago Press, 1957); George Macesich, <u>Economic Nationalism and Stability</u> (New York: Praeger, 1985);

James M. Buchanan and Gordon Tullock, The Calculus of Consent (Ann Arbor: University of Michigan Press, 1962).

6. George Macesich, "The Theory of Economic Integration and the Experience of the Balkan and Danubian Countries Before 1914," Proceedings of the First International Congress on Southeast European Studies, Sofia, Bulgaria, 1966, and F. S. U. Slavic Papers, Vol. 1 (1967); George Macesich, "Economic Theory and the Austro-Hungarian Ausgleich of 1867" [Der Osterreichisch-ungarische ausgleich, 1867], Ludovit Holitik, ed. (Bratislava: Slovak Academy, 1971); George Macesich, Geldpolitik in einem gemeinsamen europaischen markt [Money in a common-market setting] (Baden-Baden: Nomos Verlagsgesellschaft, 1972); George Macesich, "Money and a Common Market: Lessons from an Early American Experience," in Problemi privrednog razvoja i privrednog sistema jugoslavije [Problems of economic development and the economic system in Yugoslavia], Dragomir Vojnic et al. eds. (Zagreb: Globus, 1989), pp. 410-23.

I
Historical View

1

Reforms in Retrospect
Dragomir Vojnic

The economy and society of Yugoslavia underwent rapid growth and structural changes during the postwar period. In the mid-1940s, two-thirds of the overall population were engaged in farming; this had dropped to less than one-fifth by the early 1980s.

The high growth rate of the GDP from 1953-80 (6.8 percent) was achieved through high investment rates, with capital investments in the economy at 21.5 percent.

During the mid-1940s, agriculture contributed about two-fifths to the GDP, with industry at less than one-fifth. In the mid-1980s the proportions were dramatically different: Agriculture, 15 percent; industry, 42 percent.

Despite this striking developmental performance and great change, affecting the most important structural characteristics, there was a serious crisis in the late 1970s and early 1980s.

In the early 1980s the Commission of the Federal Social Councils was set up to combat the crisis and was charged with the task of producing a long-term program of economic stabilization. The commission, popularly known as the Kraigher Commission, finished its work in 1983 and published a four-volume document on its conclusions.

The commission's central document, entitled Fundamental Elements of the Long-Term Program of Economic Stabilization, deals with the nature and cause of the crisis. The document states that unfavorable developments in international environments, such as the energy crisis, overpriced dollar, and the policy of high interest rates, had aggravated the negative processes already in place in Yugoslavia because of mistakes in the country's economic and developmental policy and legislation.

Within this framework, it is important to note the mistakes of the 1980s in developmental and structural policy, which have been of special concern to economic science. A major research project in this area is entitled "Scientific Foundations of Long-Term Socioeconomic Development in Croatia and Yugoslavia," which was prepared and coordinated by the Economics Institute in Zagreb.

These documents and research findings reveal the main characteristics of Yugoslavia's concept, strategy, and development policy during the postwar years: A closed economic model and autarkic development.

The first five-year plan (1947-51) was based on the idea that Yugoslavia would participate in international economic relations and trade, which would be almost exclusively oriented toward the socialist bloc, the rest of the world being of marginal interest. However, the well-known events of 1948 drastically reversed this concept and development strategy over a very short time. The new development concept was based on export of surpluses and import substitution--the worst kind of developmental policy in both theory and practice because of its autocratic development concept.

When Yugoslavia's international standing improved, repeated attempts were made to modify this autocratic development trend through the socioeconomic reforms of 1965. These were abandoned, however, and the old trends prevailed until the 1970s.

The most determined break with this autarkic development was made in the Long-Term Program of Economic Stabilization. Although this was an ideological and theoretical break with the predominant social orientations and commitments, the economic reality was that autarkic trends were still alive and well and strong.

According to the Long-Term Program of Economic Stabilization, all of the systemic solutions, economic legislation, and economic and developmental policy measures must derive from an open economy model, with the development multipliers weighed in favor of export expansion, quality of structural changes, structural adjustments, and overall investment policy.

The greatest resistance to the implementation of such development orientation and economic, developmental, and structural policy comes from the existing structure of the Yugoslav economy, because of (1) prolonged autarkic development, (2) indexed social consciousness, and (3) dogmatic inertial attitudes. In the 1950s and 1960s, the prevailing, dogmatic view was that development concepts and strategy and long-term development policies should be planned to promote faster growth in Segment I (means of production) than in Segment II (consumer goods).

Although Yugoslav economists pointed out that such proportions applied only to the world economy, not to each individual country, this approach was influential in Yugoslav planning practices and actual development for many years. To make matters worse, this concept affected the economic structural development and market unity, not only of the Yugoslav economy, but of each constituent republic and province. This was felt most obviously in an overemphasis on quantitative criteria and sectoral priorities, such as food, energy, and raw materials to such an extent that each individual investment project overestimated the quantitative and underestimated the qualitative criteria and relations.

In strictly political-economic terms, these mistakes reflected the character and content of a subsistence economy, not a market economy. Confronted by the full force of economic logic and economic laws, the errors resulted in low efficiency, internal competitiveness, and high social development costs.

The generic expression of these failures boils down to low economic efficiency and accumulated structural problems. The range of structural problems is very broad. They include:

1. An unsatisfactory quality and quantity of participation in international trade relations and exchange, with the attendant perennial balance-of-payments and external liquidity problems;

2. A tendency for energy costs per unit of production to rise rather than fall;

3. Persistent problems of underemployment and unemployment;

4. Overestimation of the capital-intensive sectors of the economy and underestimation of the labor-intensive sectors of the economy;

5. The relatively exaggerated role for industry and neglect of the role of small-scale

business, industry, transportation, agriculture, and tourism; and

6. A whole housing and public services complex in nonsubsidized rents.

Everything impacting on the Yugoslav economy at the existing levels of integrity, soundness, and unity, or lack of them, can be classified as a structural problem. This is not a question of degrees of integration, but rather of existing relations that are predominantly determined by administrative coercion, with marginal influence from economic coercion.

Analysis points to low economic efficiency, as reflected in the nonrational management and business operations of the Yugoslav economy through massive losses. Table 1.1 illustrates this.

Table 1.1
Structure of Basic Organizations of Associated Labor (BOAL), 1978-87

	Capital Accumulation as a Percentage of Internal Reproduction Capability					
	None	Under 2	2.1-5	5.01-11	11.01-20	Over 20
1978	14.0	21.6	22.6	22.1	12.5	7.2
1979	9.8	22.3	22.8	23.6	13.5	8.0
1980	8.0	18.8	20.9	24.4	16.7	11.2
1981	7.5	18.8	20.5	24.5	17.7	11.0
1982	10.3	20.0	20.5	24.4	15.9	8.9
1983	12.0	21.3	21.4	21.7	14.4	9.2
1984	10.8	20.6	21.0	22.2	14.5	10.9
1985	11.6	23.2	20.9	21.2	13.2	9.9
1986	16.7	20.1	22.3	21.9	12.0	7.0
1987	22.1	20.1	22.8	20.3	8.9	5.8

Source: BOAL, annual balance statements, Social Accountancy Service, Belgrade.

The relevant data indicate that an increasing number of enterprises are operating either without any capital accumulation, even incurring losses, or at very low rates of capital accumulation, from 0.01 to 2 percent. These are internal rates that represent the accumulated capital left in the enterprises and the original capital used.

In 1987 over 22 percent of the enterprises operated without any accumulation, and over 20 percent with an accumulation of under 2 percent. In other words, over 40 percent of the enterprises operated without accumulation or at very low accumulation rates-- popularly known in Yugoslavia as the "positive zero." These factors have fueled the present structural inflation in Yugoslavia in a climate of "cost-push" and "demand-pull" inflationary trends. This is an important point for anyone trying to formulate an adequate market-oriented, anti-inflationary policy, since it is hard to break the inflationary trend as long as the inflation is being pushed by such great losses.

New and successful production programs offer a solution based on fresh money and the elimination of all the chronically unsuccessful operations that take losses from production. However, the other side of low efficiency is the high social cost of development. Data illustrating this are given in Table 1.2.

In Table 1.2, the social costs of development are evaluated applying the method of capital coefficients. Calculations were performed based on the Harrod-Domar macroeconomic model. The methodological foundation of the model is the well known regularity that the production growth rate expressed by the GDP is directly proportional to the rate of investment and inversely proportional to the marginal capital coefficients.

The capital coefficients show how much gross investment into fixed assets for a certain period of time is required to raise the value of production in the Yugoslav economy and industry, as expressed in the GDP, by one dinar. Both active and nonactive gross investments into fixed assets imply marginal simultaneous capital coefficients.

In 1956-60 it was necessary to spend 2.4 dinars in gross investment into fixed assets of the economy to raise the GDP by one dinar. In the subsequent five-year period (1960-65), relations worsened, and it took 2.9 dinars in gross investment into fixed assets to increase the GDP by one dinar. During the ten-year period 1960-70, the downward trend continued when the value of the capital coefficient rose to 3.6.

Table 1.2
Rates of Gross Investment in Fixed Funds,
Capital Coefficients, and GDP Growth Rates
for Industry and the Economy, 1953-86

	E C O N O M Y			I N D U S T R Y		
	Gross Invest- ment Rates (s)	Capital Coeffi- cient (k)	GDP Growth Rate (s)	Gross Invest- ments Rate (s)	Capital Coeffi- cient (k)	GDF Grov Rat (1
1953-55	20.7	1.9	10.7	59.2	4.9	12.
1956-60	18.6	2.4	7.8	31.9	2.4	13.
1961-65	19.7	2.9	6.8	32.8	3.0	10.
1956-65	19.3	2.6	7.3	32.5	3.0	11.
1966-70	20.9	3.6	5.8	31.1	5.8	5.
1971-75	20.9	3.6	5.9	29.1	3.7	7.
1966-75	21.1	3.6	5.8	30.0	3.7	6.
1976-80	24.0	4.3	5.6	33.2	4.9	6.
1976-85	20.8	6.7	3.1	26.4	4.9	4.
1981-86	17.5	15.3	1.1	20.5	7.0	2.
1953-86	20.3	3.4	5.9	28.1	3.5	8.
1953-80	21.5	3.1	6.8	32.4	3.6	9.
1953-75	20.4	2.9	7.1	31.9	3.3	9.
1953-65	19.5	2.4	8.1	35.7	3.0	12.
1956-70	20.0	2.9	6.8	31.8	3.3	9.
1961-75	30.6	5.0	6.2	30.6	3.8	8.
1961-80	21.9	3.6	6.0	31.6	4.1	7.
1971-80	22.7	4.0	5.7	31.5	4.3	7.
1976-80	20.4	6.6	3.1	26.4	5.6	4.
1966-86	20.5	4.7	4.4	26.9	4.8	5.
1956-86	20.3	3.8	5.3	27.6	3.6	7.

Source: Federal Bureau of Statistics,"Investment in
Fixed Assets, SFRY, AP 1952-1981 at 1972
Prices," Belgrade, 1983; Statisticki
godisnjak, (Belgrade, 1988); GDP and
National Income at 1972 Prices
(Belgrade). Data processing by Center
for Economic Informatics, Institute of
Economics-Zagreb.

In the precrisis period (1976-80) there was a
marked deterioration, and the capital coefficient
reached 4.3 percent. During this time, some grave
mistakes were made in economic, developmental, and

structural policies, which were compounded by the energy crisis and world recession. Yugoslavia had based its development on huge sums of borrowed money; enterprises became heavily in debt to banks and the national economy became heavily in debt to foreign creditors. As much as 20-30 percent of the overall economic investment at that time was realized with money borrowed abroad. To make matters worse, because of the misguided--and essentially dogmatic--national aversion to joint ventures, the bulk of the foreign funds was obtained in classical loans.

In the early 1980s Yugoslavia's total foreign debt was about $20 billion U.S. The debt service ratio, particularly for the convertible currency portion of the debt, fluctuated for a long time between one-third and two-fifths. Consequently, the Yugoslav economy and society found itself boxed in by overinvestment and overindebtedness in just a few years.

Overinvestment and overindebtedness have often been accused of generating the crisis; however, this view is wrong, because it confuses causes and consequences. Overinvestment and overindebtedness are the consequences; the causes run far deeper, into the developments producing the crisis in socialism. For these reasons, the solution lies in the reform of socialism.

To the question of social costs expressed as capital coefficients, it is noteworthy that in the 1980s up to 15 dinars of gross investment into fixed assets was needed to increase the GDP by one dinar.

Apart from being enormously high during the crisis years, it should be emphasized that social development costs had been very high throughout the precrisis period. A comparative analysis was performed by Aleksander Bajt (1988). A comparison of the social costs of development in Yugoslavia and four other countries with similar structural characteristics--Greece, Turkey, Spain, and Portugal--revealed that Yugoslavia's GDP could have been almost twice as high in 1980, and personal incomes even higher, if its investment efficiency had been equal to that of these other four countries over the past two decades.

The high social development costs and low economic efficiency of investments resulted in a decline in qualitative factors and overall development quality. This is particularly noticeable in the deterioration of relations between production factors and technological advancement as contributors to the GDP growth rate of the economy.

A more subtle analysis performed for the project, entitled "The Strategy of Technological Development of Yugoslavia 'till the Beginning of the Twenty-First Century," was performed by Ante Puljic of the Economics Institute (Zagreb). Puljic's analysis confirms these findings in Table 1.3.

Table 1.3
GDP Growth Rates of the Economy: Contributions of Production Factors and Technological Advancement

	$\dfrac{Q}{100\ Q}$	$\dfrac{L}{100a\ L}$	$\dfrac{K}{100b\ K}$	$100c$	$\dfrac{cQ}{100\ Q}$
1965-84	5.0	1.9	1.9	1.2	24.(
1965-74	6.4	1.5	2.7	2.2	34.‹
1975-84	2.8	2.2	0.4	0.2	7..

Q = GDP
L = effective working hours
K = fixed assets employed
a = elasticity of production with labor
b = elasticity of production with fixed assets
c = rate of natural progression of technological advancement

Source: Ante Puljic, Veza izmedju tehnoloskog razvoja, privrednog sistema i ekonomske politike (The relation between technological development, economic system, and economic policy) (Zagreb: Economics Institute, 1987), p. 18. Statistical data processing by the Center for Informatics and Statistics, Economics Institute-Zagreb.

Contributions to the technological advancement of the GDP growth rate of the economy dropped from 34.4 percent in 1965-74 to only 7.1 percent in 1975-84. As the crisis intensified in the 1980s, these relations rapidly deteriorated, although the quality of industrial development was slightly higher. Relevant data are presented in Table 1.4.

Table 1.4
GDP Growth Rates in Industry:
Contributions by Production Factors and
Technological Advancement

	$100\dfrac{Q}{Q}$	$100a\dfrac{L}{L}$	$100b\dfrac{K}{K}$	$100c$	$100\dfrac{cQ}{Q}$
1965-84	5.5	1.3	2.3	1.9	34.5
1965-74	6.5	0.5	2.5	3.5	53.8
1975-84	4.7	1.7	2.1	0.9	19.1

Q = GDP
L = effective working hours
K = fixed assets employed
a = elasticity of production with labor
b = elasticity of production with fixed assets
c = rate of natural progression of technological
advancement

Source: Ante Puljic, <u>Veza izmedju tehnoloskog razvoja, privrednog sistema i ekonomske politike</u> (The relation between technological development, economic system, and economic policy) (Zagreb: Economics Institute, 1987), p. 18. Statistical data processing by the Center for Informatics and Statistics, Economics Institute-Zagreb.

During the ten-year period 1965-74, the contribution by technological advancement to the GDP growth rate of industry was 53.8 percent; however, it dropped to only 19.1 percent in 1975-84.

A marked deterioration in these relations occurred in the crisis period of 1981-84, when technological advancement contributions to the GDP growth rate dropped to only 3.8 percent.

In the context of the present analysis, the most important conclusion is that errors in the application of economic laws to concepts, development strategy, and long-term development policy resulted in low levels of economic efficiency, high social costs of development strategy, and unsatisfactory quality of development, along with unmet structural changes and applications. It is not surprising, then, that a crisis developed. Economic laws state that long-term development and structural policies can succeed when predicated on these two strategic assumptions.

1. An open economy model with development multipliers to focus on export expansion instead of import substitution; and

2. The development of the country's own fundamental knowledge and new technologies for the development and production of new products and the linkage of scientific research and development is a prerequisite for a successful and creative transfer of technology, along with continuous work on development strategy.

In all of the rhetoric thus far about the reforms to socialism and the Yugoslav developmental experience, no adequate concept and development strategy has been devised by anyone, because such a concept and development strategy begin with quantitative criteria and sectoral priorities, such as food, raw materials, and energy, with allocations of accumulated capital based on these priorities. The result of proceeding without a sound strategy has been mistakes, inefficiency, high social costs of development, and finally a crisis.

A modern, dynamic, and scientifically based policy and development strategy should begin with qualitative criteria, making quantitative criteria and sectoral priorities subordinate to it. This further implies that it should build on (1) an open economy model, (2) integral market functions, (3) predominant economic coercion, (4) technological and energy development defined on this basis, (5) indicative planning, and (6) diversified measures on economic developmental policy and on all other segments of the economic environment.

2

Socialism: Illusion and Reality
Ljubisav Markovic

When socialism entered history, it was to be a solution to the conflicts of the human past and a projection for the future, based on scientific thought, and hence irrefragable. It was this perception that nurtured the fervor of generations, the ideals of intellectuals, and the general aspirations of people for justice and equality. It was under these banners that revolutions and profound politico-economic change took place in a number of countries in the twentieth century.

However, as with many movements of the past, the irony of history has not spared socialist revolutions. Human ideals have once again been exposed to the mockery of cruel social practice, and intended reform in economics, politics, and ethics has been turned upside down. In this last decade of the twentieth century, it is clear that official socialism has been discredited and that its theoretical and political critique must be undertaken without delay. All the facets of the socialist system must be examined, without any fetishes being made of its fundamental or overall values. Nothing should be exempt: not the doctrine socialism employs to effect changes in political power, not property in that economic order, and not the individual within that overall social setup.

Yugoslav socialism found itself in the same historical context, as international socialism, <u>Mutatis</u> <u>mutandis</u>. As early as the 1950s, social processes were set in motion that aimed for a different system, geared toward producer power and direct democracy. This was attended by extensive political and theoretical debate, which tended to refute the sacrosanct postulates of socialism and broaden its social vistas. The general debate made a brilliant critique of state socialism and brought an awareness of the inevitability of objective social laws, primarily those of commodity production and capital; however, at the same time many illusions crept into this theoretical arsenal about the economics and politics of self-management. The worker was held to have miraculous power when he "controls" income; the Communist Party was therefore to be accorded monolithic position and rule. This ideology set the stage for a total social and economic fiasco in a truly ubiquitous bureaucracy.

Apparently the nature of crisis in a socialist society or law is difficult to grasp, and its limitations tend to be overlooked, as is generally the case with those who rule and are being ruled. In fact, this accounts for the longevity of the crisis and the credulous assumption that one or another imaginative reform move or "this or that" measure to remedy the economy, the market position, or the federation would finally result in prosperity and peace--the "good old times" kind of peace.

Political thinkers still fail to realize the whole truth about the causes of the social crisis and the profundity of the inevitable changes in the ruling communist power, which still harbors the illusion that democracy will lend itself to a degree of adaptation. Numerous scientific works have discussed issues like social property in great detail, but apparently with little real impact.

Naturally, the ruling political establishment is not indifferent to the unrest in society and the quandaries that stem not only from the profound crisis in the economy but also from the establishment's own political conflicts. The establishment is fully active, constantly implementing rational and austere programs and designing economic and political reforms. None the less, it remains pragmatic, true to itself and the foundations of its control over society, which is the secret of its past failures in various socialist reforms. With the announcement of free enterprise, private property, a market economy, and democracy, what does the future hold? It is still too early to tell.

The new project of economic and political reform also involves scientific circles. However, an omnipresent question is that of the limits of scientific influence. At what point does scientific thought challenge the foundations of the political establishment? How does it maintain its power and the range of its social influence over the lives of people?

The state and the political establishment have acquired new social power and significance in contemporary society. This has to be seen as a legitimate process, even actual progress in the function of productive forces, as well as in the socialization of wealth produced. Basically, this process is a general one that grows in the soil of developed capitalism and in other areas as well.

Socialist revolutions have provided the foundation for this historical trend, acting radically in the full sense of the word. In keeping with political doctrine, they have produced a total turnabout in the character of the state and in its authority over social processes. State authority has become all-embracing, controlling the political and economic resources of society and the actions of its people, even their thinking.

Stalin saw this new might and function of the state as the principal lever in the construction of socialism. His perception was correct, which explains the potentials, the vagaries, and the limits of the promised socialism up to the current general crisis.

However, Stalin is not original in his doctrine of the central authority of the state in socialism. This political doctrine had already been enunciated by Karl Marx in some of his contemplative excursions, where he ceased to be an economic theoretician and shifted to the domain of political adventure. Still Stalin deserves a place in history, as he was a dedicated follower of Marx and implemented the demands of communism in his radical Asian way.

State authority has its theoretical genesis in socialist thought, but it is also a long tradition. Its actual dimensions are determined by (1) state authority over total social capital and human labor, or social property as the sole legitimate property, and (2) the communist party as the only legitimate political vanguard in the system and as an integral element of the state, the economy, and the culture and the police/army of the entire social order.

Again, state authority emanates from capitalism but undergoes a transformation and changed social position during a crisis. As a political lever of the bourgeoisie--its auxiliary instrument--the state becomes an independent politico-economic power, gaining supremacy in society over all classes and levels of society. The actual basis for this power and function of the state stems from the needs inherent in the social nature of production and capital formation, not to be measured by the extent of capital nationalization. It is to be seen as a historical need of progressive production. The economic power of the state rests upon a developed scientific economics and a system of practical incentives and safeguards to the stability of private interests, capital, and economic and social prosperity at large.

The independent social position of the capitalist state rests upon its strategic responsibility to capital accumulation or responsibility for economic growth and the employment of the population. John Maynard Keynes and other thinkers, like John Galbraith and Paul Samuelson, have given an economic analyses of these processes.

Official socialism refutes the economic and sociological changes in the relationship between the state and the economy and the progressive significance of these changes or the convergence of contemporary social processes. This is out of practical class instinct. It occurs when the ruling bureaucracy spontaneously decides that recognition of convergence threatens its mission of being the true agent for happiness in the new world--it is a revolution brought on by the bureaucracy, rather than by the erratic social progress of capitalism.

The same economic and social processes promote bureaucracy in politics and in the state. On that score, socialism need have no doubts, for it is definitely superior to capitalism. Total state ownership and a general political and ideological communist-party monopoly of society mean absolute authority. The party/state is transformed into an omnipotent ruler of society, regardless of how much flirting with democracy and economics there many be. In other words, the contemporary structure of socialism necessarily breeds a bureaucracy of the political establishment and of all relations and institutions in the state. Although a resolution of these issues, bringing socialism back to the province of economics and democracy, has yet to be found, it remains a hope for the future.

After all the upheavals intended to secure rule by the workers--the producers--the Yugoslav social system still remains state socialism, with omnipotent political echelons. This is a bitter realization in light of everything that has happened in the political field and in light of the brilliant theoretical works. Still, it should come as no surprise given all the events on the Yugoslav social scene, where the interest of the party-state force is just one of the factors.

The shift of focus to the economy and the producer makes history in itself and certainly cannot be effected overnight; it also brings to light fresh contradictions and ideological challenges. Political aspirations alone will not suffice for this, nor will massive creative endeavor, no matter how fruitful. Without the framework of the material and cultural circumstances of Yugoslavia, the inertia of the socialist illusions of the people, and the new social relations/conflicts, there is fertile ground for conflict in the political movement. In fact, it is well-known, even inevitable, that every new order is attended by ideological or scientific misconceptions.

In Yugoslavia, the social processes of the 1970s are mirrored in these scenarios.

1. The political establishment definitely cast the worker as an "untouchable" socialist, the principal social official. That worker was to enter into various economic and political associations for decisions on the means and affairs of social production.

2. The worker, associated labor, and the income the worker allegedly controlled and used for his immediate and broader interests was to become the linchpin of society and a political maxim. The entire structure of the economic system, the deployment of authority, and the institutions of culture and health were to be derived from this political vehicle.

3. Most of the scientific establishment and political circles considered this worker status to be a solution to the contradictions of socialism and a definitive end for state socialism, creating a foolproof barrier against political voluntariness and bureaucracy. With worker-controlled incomes and the necessary motivation to do business efficiently, there was to be rational product use, which was to bring accumulation, general prosperity, and democracy.

However, the socialist zeal was short-lived, as in reality, everything became quite the opposite. Economic efficiency dwindled, and so did the rate of capital formation. On the other hand, numerous state and parastate institutions cropped up, in a veritable state-structured hypertrophy. This was compounded by

31

a complicated, sterile, and costly decisionmaking procedure and by the indifference of workers to capital and accumulation. A wave of bureaucracy, parasitism, and spending engulfed all political institutions, work organizations, and the economy proper in education, health, culture, and science.

Some of the illusions of the 1970s lingered for a while, or as long as the abundant flow of foreign capital kept making up for the internal economic decline. Foreign loans and the inflow of savings by the workers concealed the real truth. But the 1980s brought major upheavals and uncertainties; the country itself was in a not so clearly defined crisis of monumental proportions, which continued into the 1990s.

The social order of the 1970s only enhanced the importance of political factors and administrations. Politics became uncircumventable, not only in the ideological and legal areas but also in internal social production relations. It could not have been otherwise with total state ownership and the compartmentalization of social capital--up to the worker and the specific needs of economic and political institutions. Only total political authority or the political establishment, with all the bureaucracy and voluntariness it entails, could sustain the internal life of society, keep it meaningful and within bounds. But voluntariness, especially in a crisis, was also the faith of the communist party in its own socialism, which was bursting at the seams. The decaying social fabric was falling apart from the tension caused by the emerging material of human growth and potential.

The communist order--socialism is disintegrating in all its forms and concepts. What is really falling apart is the rule of the Communist Party. No special analysis is needed to note that this process begins at a given high level of industry and culture, engendered by wealth and human aspirations rather than by poverty; this is a symptom and also a warning. Evidently, the contradictions of the system and its crises have deeper roots; they do not stem solely from the political monopoly of the Communist Party. The party ruled for a long period, to bring significant social progress despite certain political excesses. However, general social crisis is a phenomenon of our times.

Thus, the question now is why rule by the Communist Party is viewed as something anachronous, conservative, and on a collision course with human progress--at odds with history. This question requires discussion and debate. To begin with, the concept of Communist Party rule, social content, and historical importance have to be examined.

The social content of that rule is complex, and we have already addressed the principal social-structure segments in which the party has a leading role. The party regulates the anatomy and physiology of the social being everywhere, as an internal control panel. It operates in all quarters as an agent of a higher power and surfaces publicly when there are disruptions in the economy or on the political scene, but only it is inviolable.

The concept that the position of the Communist Party is one of a political-authority monopoly lacks completeness: It leaves out the essence. The party is to be seen as a embodiment of production relations in the Yugoslav order. That is the most important characteristic and the real basis of its social power, which is a hidden feature, but one common to all communist states. Countries differ in many ways, and with worker self-management, Yugoslavia is no exception.

The entire process of social production is permeated by the authority of the Communist Party, subordinated to its doctrine of socialism, its judgments, and its policy. That is a significant fact, regardless of the infinite variety of institutions and formal democratic management forms. Total social property signifies the total rule, or total or dominant significance, of the Communist Party over the material existence of institutions and people. Apparently, rule by the party has stratified society to an extent that capitalism can never achieve. On the one hand, we have the monopolistic owner of the means of production and social wealth, which is the Communist Party, and on the other, we have all of society as a hired-labor subject. Anyone who finds himself outside of this monopolized system of production relations can perhaps save his skin but hardly his social identity. That identity tends to be lost, especially if the person happens to do something wrong in the eyes of the official interpreters of socialism and moral integrity.

Even the issue of the relationship between the party and the state should be seen from this angle. A monopoly over the state is not an ordinary monopoly over the state force. The true meaning of this monopoly is that it covers the economic functions of the state, either totally or partially--it is total economic control over society and over any significant social function.

Regarding power in the system of social production relations, the importance of democratic centralism certainly stands, but so do a number of sociological phenomena: the subservience to communists, bureaucracy, careerism, denunciation, and lack of vision. When compared to this whole inquisition, the idea that democratic centralism towered above it was a European joke. The genuine quintessence of the social and personal power of the Communist Party is a calcified mechanism, and woe is he who incurs its wrath. Apart from deep social scars, there is often the loss of means to support a family.

State ownership of the means of production and democratic centralism are instrumental in the social omnipotence of communist rule, which spawned numerous disruptions and fomented a general crisis that has no certain solutions.

Critical remarks placing the Communist Party in the focus of social productive relations need to be supplemented, because this social symbiosis is not fortuitous but is rather a legal or historically rational development given to individual countries at that time--an example is Yugoslavia. At a certain juncture, it became part of the general system of capitalism but featured a few of its own economic and social structure elements. According to research papers and actual facts, Yugoslavia later adopted capitalism as an appendage of its imperialistic epoch, when she had to bear all of the exploitation hardships of capitalism without having its rate of capital formation. With this background, developments with this end, economic inertia, and social torpor were inevitable. In other words, an anticapitalist, socialist revolution was only logical, and it was inspired and undertaken by the Communist Party as its great national exploit. A different political rule in social character, involving the nationalization of economic resources and of means/labor, marked only the first step in the strategy of profound transformation--the building of socialism. Soon a number of thinkers harbored the suspicion that what was emerging was instead a process of primitive accumulation of capital. Needless to say, socialism definitely played its chosen role in this process. With every new five-year plan, it sustained enthusiasm about better days to come, and it undertook compulsory humane and enlightened policy programs. However, in real life there were constant cruelties and primitive capital accumulation laws, supported by the boundless faith of the masses in the Communist Party and its programs for the future. Worker self-management particularly reinforced this bond, dispelling any suspicions about the ideological "rightness" of the order.

Laws governing the primitive accumulation of capital led to a logical development of the social system: a merging of the Communist Party with production relations. The idyllic moments of this primitive accumulation, accompanied by the ubiquitous pompousness and endless string of interminable investment projects, included (1) forcible concentration and state centralization of capital; (2) mobilization of labor quotas; (3) forced generation of surplus value; (4) revision of the surplus of agricultural produce, rural exodus, a general plan-based distribution, rationing, and living on the breadline and below; and (5) migration to the cities and construction of new cities. These projects were possible only because they were backed by the untouchable revolutionary authority of the Communist Party, with its state-sanctioned violence and its all-embracing daily action. The egalitarianism of a poor nation and its communist practices at the workplace and in education and health, along with the ethics and moral principles of the communists--all seemed immaculate, an almost magnificent vision.

The communist order and party rule as a production relation are of generally progressive significance to a certain level of society, despite all of the manipulations and bureaucratic greed of politicians that a historian can ferret out. Capital was created; industrial activity was set in motion; many generations received an education; and broad communications with the rest of the world were established.

There was a flare-up of contradictions when the time became ripe to introduce different economic and social forms--different ways to regulate the status of urban and rural areas and the position of the state/communist power. The glaring contradictions eroded trust in all institutions, including the state, and coincided with vascillation and self-delusion in the ranks of the political leadership. The extensive crisis was compounded by a reluctance to sober up, both in the minds of the people and in bureaucratized social practice. Moreover, the facts warn us that the transformation of primitive communism into a state of the normal accumulation of capital and democracy will be a genuine historical challenge, more complex than the challenges of the past, under a rural and patriarchal Yugoslavia. At that stage, slogans and promises of a secure future were no longer sufficient.

Thus, even the political establishment is torn by a conflict between different, truly contradictory and antagonistic--periods that, rather than establishing continuity for the revolution, are its criticism, refutation, and discontinuity. This conflict is behind the political disputes about relations in the social system of the country and the exclusiveness of political movements and personal intolerance. Hence, it is not a question of misunderstanding or one-sidedness.

That the economic and social laws governing the primitive or normal accumulation of capital vary is a scientifically established fact. Coercion is the main ingredient in the primitive accumulation of capital. Reference should be made to the economic analyses of these processes in England, as undertaken by Marx. "Force is the midwife of any old society, which carries a new society in its womb." It is force that destroys the old ownership and social structure and drives peasants away from the land en masse, denying them the opportunity to earn a living in agriculture and placing them in industrial workshops. This is how cities are created, determined by each country's history and the availability of hired labor.

In Yugoslavia, socialist humaneness has been intertwined with harsh truths, now coming to light. In England, sheep drive the peasants from their land; in Yugoslavia, both peasants and goats were banished. What a drama could be written about the slaughter of goats--the chief source of livelihood for many families. Then there was the plundering of common pastures by the state. This was basically as summarized by Karl Marx: "The basis of this entire process is the expropriation of the agricultural producer, the peasant from his land. Its history varies from country to country . . . and from historical epoch to epoch."

But we are not dealing with our history here, but rather with the nature of the primitive social order. Its basic features include (1) a unitaristic party state; (2) state ownership; (3) democratic centralism and obeisant political discipline; (4) state-hired laborers and state subjects/citizens; (5) and egalitarianism--personal, but also across-the-board socialist--in the territorial distribution of capital and consumption.

It is understood that normal, economic accumulation of capital requires a different type and character of state. _Inter alia_, its ownership and social prerogatives have to be constricted in favor of economic, political, educational, and other institutions and entities. These are linked to the system of social production based on market logic and private interests. Even what is necessarily a function of the contemporary state, such as economic, scientific, educational, and welfare strategies, has to be controlled by free political forces or citizens in a democratic process.

Evidently the Communist Party failed to appreciate this classical succession of historical periods. It failed to transform itself, to perceive on time the limitations of its doctrine or the limits of its control over production relations and the state. Its nonchalant statism and democratic centralism have bureaucratized and dogmatized its practice until it is an impediment to further social progress. Its thought has remained stereotypical, and its practice is devoid of political initiative, especially in environments with unfavorable normal accumulation of capital.

This prolongs the crisis in society and the agony of the communist order, which began in the late 1960s. The crisis worsened in the 1970s, while in the 1980s the system collapsed, and general uncertainty has followed.

Changing a given social system, especially when it will inevitably transform its true character, is certainly not an automatic process, notwithstanding erratic developments and marked contraditions in society. While many factors are involved in this process, ideas and people are critically important.

However, it is now quite clear that our age calls for ideas that will not be copies of the enlightenment of the eighteenth century or of the freethinking ideals of the bourgeois revolutions. We are dealing with a different human technological power, different kinds of state functions, a different market, different laws governing man's socialization, and different positions for science and democracy.

Inter alia, democracy is no longer a mechanism to gain social benefits and appropriate profit, or a mechanism to assign individuals to important offices, but rather a way of placing emphasis on social programs to promote a given character of the social order, within the framework of the same ownership and political structure of society. The Communist Party has overlooked this fact. Since the late 1960s, it has been guided by a number of insular ideas, unaware

37

of their outworn character. It fully relied on the
strength of its over 2 million party members, its
tentacles infiltrating all institutions, and its
democratic centralism by which the dictates of the
leadership would be binding on all without fail. All
of this has led to discredit, demoralization,
anarchy, and collapse.

The social system in Yugoslavia does have a chance
to avoid devastating disintegration processes and to
carry out a less painful but necessary
metamorphosis.   That chance stems from the
advantages offered by self-management as an economic
and political part of its communities.   But here
again, we are not dealing with worker self-management
as a socialist method of managing the economy. This
was an illusion that misled both workers and the
public at large, and even the highest echelons of the
Communist Party. Worker self-management, if we
disregard its genesis, is a lucky break for us,
because it has a different kind of historical
character. Without an in-depth analysis of this,
there are the following indicators:

1. Worker   self-management   as   a link   between
    workers and the means of production through
    machine technology.

2. It is a form of private (collective) ownership
    by the workers over their (social) capital.

3. It is a form of socialization of the mode of
    commodity production, of the state, and of the
    market, that is, of the modern social labor
    productivity potential. The self-management
    practices of German concerns illustrate this
    better than all of the trade union archives in
    Yugoslavia put together.

3

Transition Problems
Rikard Lang

THE ISSUE

The transition to a market economy is unfolding in a number of countries, and that transition is one of the most important economic issues of today. Although this transition is of course most prominent in Central and Eastern Europe, it is not limited to this geographic area, and it bears the effects of previous attempts at reform in goals, principles, methods, institutions, and instruments. Discussions on systemic changes and market plans have persisted in these countries for decades. In addition, the countries in transition debate privatization and changes in the ownership structure.

The essentials of the economic system are in the research, conceptualization, and implementation stages. New interactions began with the political systems, which are also undergoing transformation. Experience has proved that this process of reform is indeed a precondition of the current transition from one economic system to a new one, and that the process will continue after this transition is made.

These changes stimulate a new area of comparative research known as "transitional economics." During this identification of problems and search for solutions in these economies, a new body of insights emerges to form the building blocks of a theory of transition with explanatory and predictive value. In the context of this chapter, the term <u>transition</u> refers to the process of change from any type of command to a market economy. This type of transition is a new phenomenon, with a new set of problems. The solutions to these problems cannot be found in previous experience or accepted theory.

In an approach to the dynamics of systemic changes, it is necessary to distinguish adjustments and reforms from transition to a new system. Systemic changes were prominent in Yugoslavia after World War II, as revealed in the economic literature. Yugoslavia began her departure from a previously predominant command economy around 1950, considerably earlier than economies in Central and Eastern Europe. A separate path was taken on important systemic changes, and its economic system began to evolve differently. This being so, then why did not the transition to a modern market economy begin earlier?

Yugoslavia's economic system is currently engaged in a transition process that goes beyond the economic sphere. As in other countries of the region, the choices in the establishment and evolution of the economic system, a central issue in the transition, have been made in the past under the prevailing influence of a one-party political system and the resulting relations among the political organization, the state, and the economy. The makeup of the economic system is a result of the political environment. Ideological preferences and political considerations are also decisive in economic decisions.

However, the gradual demand for essential changes increased, especially since Yugoslavia needed, and still needs, to extricate herself from a long-range crisis that is not limited to the economic process. The crisis includes the entire framework of society-- its identity, credibility, legitimacy, integration, and participation. Never the less, the crisis in the political, legal, and social system is closely intertwined with the economic problems.

The long-lasting crisis has led to the conclusion that any possible positive effect of impact by the prevailing economic model on the rational function of the economy and its development potential were exhausted. The widely held view is that this economic model has not offered an institutional framework that is adequate to drive the economy in a changing internal and external environment.

The present transition to a new economic system presents new problems, which are just entering economic theory and the practice of economic systems. Yugoslavia is in the grips of radical changes, having already undergone, in a historically short period of time, a succession of economic reforms and experiments not shared by other countries of the region. The continuing discussion of a market plan began earlier in the search for a proper economic system.

How does the evolution of the economic system in

Yugoslavia affect the present transition to a new economic system? Gustan Ranis reminds us that all economies move along ambiguous, uncertain, and non-monotonic paths, lurching forward or sideways or partially retracing their steps. His observation also applies to the emerging economic system in Yugoslavia.

Central and Eastern Europe are now involved in transition from one to an essentially different economic system, and from types of command to market economies. Institutional problems of transition were primarily centered on economic development; research was not so much concentrated on the transition problems from one economic system to a different one. Now, numerous questions are asked about the way the past and the changes in environment will impact the concepts and implementation of the present transition to market economies. What will be the results of the change in political system to parliamentary democracy, now in progress in these countries? Under these circumstances, what insights into the general transition problems, their identification, and their solutions can be offered to facilitate implementation of a theory of transition? Because no theory actually exists for this type of transition, a limited discussion will focus on Yugoslavia here.

CONCEPTS

Some concepts, such as those of the economic system, economic reform, and the transition from a command to a market economy, are the building blocks in a discussion of transition problems in Yugoslavia. They are not unanimously adopted nor is there a general consensus about the key issue, which is the economic system. The approach is determined by the purpose to be served. In the context of this paper, two definitions are useful. M. Montias (1976) offers an abstract definition, treating economic systems as institutional frameworks designed by social preferences that determine the function and development of an economy. An economic system is composed of economic, political, and social institutions, organizations, laws, rules, and values interacting with other subsystems of the socioeconomic system to affect the economy through production, distribution, exchange, and consumption.

Instead of presenting abstract explanations, J. Kornai (1986) offers a summary of the main components of an economic system:

- The organizations functioning in the economy

- The distribution of the various forms of ownership and property rights

- The distribution of the decisionmaking power

- The information structure

- The types of information flowing between organizations

- The incentives motivating the decisionmakers

- The role of political organs and the government in economic affairs

- The laws and governmental resolutions or the formal legal regulation of the economy's operations

- The informal "rules of the game"

- The routine behavioral patterns complementing the formal legal regulation.

Some definitions emphasize that an economic system is a set of evolving social relations, with historical roots and different phases. This process is not without conflict, power struggles, and resistance to change as it unfolds in the various stages.

The concept of the economic system here is interwoven with preferred economic and noneconomic outcomes. These result not only from the nature of the economic system and its actual function but also from the environment and from policies. The dynamic character of economic systems is prominent in the transition from one system to an essentially different one. The complexity of the actual transition from a command to a market economy involves all of the components of the economic system of a country.

If there is to be efficient function and development of an economy, the economic system must be able to adjust to pressures. Accordingly, in the evaluation of economic systems, adaptability is a criterion. Systems are considered to be flexible if they can adjust in content, impact, and costs, and do so in a socially acceptable and preferred manner. This is quite impossible in rigid, static, and inefficient systems.

Economic reform is directly connected with change. Some definitions seem very broad, not distinguishing reforms from general adjustments and the specific dynamic processes involved. Different types of economic reforms are known, whether partial or comprehensive. Some argue that radical economic reforms constitute a special type of adjustment, because they change the function of the economic system, especially through the economic subjects and their relationships with the environment.

The dynamic character of economic systems is prominent in an analysis of the transition from one economic system to another. At present, it refers to the transition from a command to a market economy.

This transition is a novel phenomenon, impossible within the framework of a pretransition system. The new type of systemic and political change now occurring in Central and Eastern Europe is complex and requires a long-term process. Since there is no theoretical foundation for this process at present, it is a learning process.

Because of its complexity, this transition requires that each country involved make a strategy choice. An important issue in reform strategy is the pace of the transformation, whether it should be rapid or gradual. Andras Simon (1990) suggests that the Hungarian way is typically a gradual strategy, whereas Poland's strategy is considered by some authors to be fast-paced.

The quick strategy brings about a fast transition to a market economy. This is characterized by the introduction of (1) a convertible national currency, (2) private company establishments, (3) commercial loans, (4) changes in the tax system, (5) abolition of price controls, and (6) elimination of soft budget constraints. While transition strategies vary by country, it appears that Yugoslavia prefers a quick strategy.

A transition to a fundamentally different economic system occurs in phases, as a metamorphic phenomenon. The characteristic phases depend in high degree on the chosen stragegy, with constraints driven significantly by institutional changes, which can promote or inhibit the transition process.

Among transitional problems are the choices of economic institutions, especially in the transitional phases. These choices involve (1) the institutions' efficiency, (2) the rigidity of their institutional posture, (3) the predictability of their institutional changes, and (4) the costs of these changes. These areas are among the research topics of the new institutional economics. Although the interest of this new branch of economics has hitherto been centered on development problems, its application to the dynamics of transition to a different economic system is promising.

In Yugoslavia the dynamics of the economic system in the transitional phase are tied to institutional changes, which confront specific issues after a period of institutional experiment.

DYNAMICS OF THE ECONOMIC SYSTEM

The transitional problems of economic systems depend on the specifics of an economy. The configuration of the transitional problems in an economy is the result of numerous factors, such as the level of economic development, the previous changes, the present character of the economic system, the type of political system, and the constitutional arrangements. Insight into the dynamics of an economic system requires enormous information about its beginning and about its transition goals, to explain the rationale of resistances and obstacles to change.

Some transition problems are rooted in the economic system. Analyzing these contributes to an understanding of the issues in the actual transition in Yugoslavia.

After World War II, history had left this country an inheritance that became a fertile ground for disagreement and conflicts over changes in the economic system.

Yugoslavia is a multinational country with differences in history, traditions, languages, religions, and cultures. When Yugoslavia was constituted in the aftermath of World War II, these differences did not disappear into a melting pot of togetherness. The multinational character of the country had an important impact on the present transition problems. In the last official census, in 1981, the Serbs (36.3 percent) and the Croats (19.8 percent) accounted for more than half of the population, about 12.6 million. The natural growth rates of the different nationalities varies considerably; and the population is changing rapidly.

Yugoslavia is a federation composed of six republics and two autonomous regions. There is a characteristically persistent north/west-south/east division in its level of economic development, a division that did not change in spite of the general industrialization, urbanization, and modernization after World War II. The development levels of the different regions tend to coincide with national concentrations, and this is indeed an aggravating factor in a multinational country.

According to UN data, Yugoslavia compares with Western European countries at a low level of economic development. The economic growth rate varied significantly and manifested a negative trend throughout the 1980s. The average per capita rate of GNP growth (material concept) amounted to 4.2 percent from 1948 to 1988 and decreased to -.02 percent between 1981 and 1982.

This factual background contributes to an explanation of the changes in the economic system. Although distinct phases in the evolution of this system are apparent, they are not strictly separated. Nonetheless, milestones are obvious in the history of Yugoslavia's economic reforms and of the adjustments within the same economic system.

This history of economic reforms begins with the transition from a war economy and the aftermath of World War II to a centralized command economy with the introduction of a basically Soviet-type economic model, which affected the whole economic system. It was intertwined with the constitution of a single-party political system, with close ties between the state, the party, and the economy. This transition evolved over a short period of time in a normative way, although the social costs of the transition have not been systematically assessed.

Such a transition could also be witnessed in other countries of Central and Eastern Europe during his time. The character of the transition depended mostly on the environment of change and whether or not it was made under the pressure of foreign intervention. Many traits of this socioeconomic system have proved to be very persistent and have been met at different junctures on the tortuous road leading to the evolution of a new economic system.

The Yugoslav departure from this system, the first break from it in Central and Eastern Europe, started in the early 1950s. It marked the beginning of a wave of economic reforms, initiated by the appearance of ideas about worker self-management and experimental attempts to implement it.

Different groups of changes can be chosen to delineate the different phases of the reform process. These milestones offer insights into the present transition problems:

- The beginning of the departure from the central model

- The 1965 social and economic reform

- The mid-1970s reform

- The 1981 Long-Term Program of Economic Stabilization

- The transition of the 1990s

The departure from the command economy was mainly done for political considerations. It spawned a creeping self-management movement lacking any historical experience and theoretical basis. A critique of Stalinism reveals its lingering influence on (1) the economy and society, (2) the early experiences with worker self-management, and (3) the growing economic difficulties.

The reforms of 1965 were powered by inflation, economic instability, economically unwarranted regional differences, and a technology lag, along with the noneconomic impact. The 1965 reform failed and was finally abandoned without analysis, in spite of its significance to the dynamics of the economic system, to later reforms, and to the transition of the 1990s.

Another facet of the 1965 reform was the devolution of authority radiating from the federal center to the republics. The shortcomings of this change became the basis for a new type of centralization. The autonomy of the enterprises with self-management and the role of the market mechanism were an essential feature of the reform. A critical evaluation of the chosen development stategy resulted in the recommendation of an export-oriented economy or an attempted transition to some form of open, market-oriented economy. However, many remnants of the old system remained.

Changes to the political system were not considered in 1965. Resistance to reform ideas came in the form of criticism of liberalism, technology, and nationalism--phenomena allegedly having a negative effect on political and economic development. The 1965 reform highlighted some real problems in the transition to a market economy, but it did not solve them.

The economic reform of the mid-1970s attempted to

implement the principle of comprehensive self-management. It was anticipated that associated labor would be the general principle and basis for an institutional framework of self-management and decisionmaking. A new system of economic categories was established to introduce a consensus economy. Aggreement and compacts were expected to perform limited basic market functions in the absence of capital and labor markets. Because of problems with the economic system, the role of the state in economic decisionmaking increased. This utopian economic reform induced a regression in the evolvement of the economic system, contributing to the unsatisfactory performance of the economy in the 1980s.

In 1981 the mounting pressure of economic difficulties forced a comprehensive evaluation of market function. Its outcome was a reform project, the Long-Term Program of Economic Stabilization, which witnessed the maturing of reform thinking. Although not implemented when expected, it was an important forerunner of the transition of the 1990s, as it offered insights into the agonizing road leading from utopia to reality.

This reform program contained an incisive critique of past concepts of the rise of the economic system and of economic policy choices. It was a comprehensive program highlighting new vistas of a market role in the economy and emphasizing the transition to an open economy.

This reform, although not implemented after its publication and formal acceptance in 1983, met with mainly political resistance. It should not be regarded as an abortive program, however, since its ideas strongly influenced later reform, and it can be considered an important link in the evolution of reform thinking.

There were different phases in the departure from the centralized administrative system. The actual changes were not unidirectional. Common threads running through this time were (1) the normative way the economic system evolved and (2) the recurring themes in the unfolding process of reform thinking, such as autonomy of enterprises, the market role, changes in development strategy, and transition to an open economy. All of these goals met with resistance.

Could reform thinking in Yugoslavia be considered naive? The naivete of the reformers appeared in different guises, through expectations pinned to (1) the limited market mechanism as an isolated phenomenon, (2) self-management, (3) administrative decentralization, and (4) reforms introduced from "above" that disregarded broadly shared preferences. Did the reformers loose their naivete during the forty years of the transformation process, or is it still present in the changes envisioned for the transition of the 1990s?

TRANSITION IN THE 1990s

In the early 1990s in Central and Eastern Europe, the terms <u>transitional economics</u> and <u>problems of transition</u> received a special connotation of broader changes than economic reform, although the new features of the economic systems are of central importance. The kind of transition implied cannot be achieved within the existing economic systems and refers to specific transformations of entire socioeconomic systems. It is mainly defined as a transition from command to market economies, and it is closely intertwined with the political systems. The constituent elements of this transition--the strategies, the institutions, forms, and costs--are also influenced by the particular nature of each country.

In the early 1990s in Yugoslavia, the concept of a transition to a new economic system has been nurtured in a climate of deep economic, political, and social crisis, which have contributed to an onslaught of anachronistic dogmas and proposed utopias. The economic crisis was manifested through hyperinflation, internal and external indebtedness, structural disproportions, and a widening technological gap. These produced an environment of social, political, and national disagreement and conflict, which is not surprising in Yugoslavia, a multinational country.

The leading forces driving the present changes are pressures generated by the prolonged economic crisis and by the inability to resolve growing conflicts within the existing system. There is a broadly shared view that the main goals of the transformation--economic efficiency and a stable democracy--can be reached only through the transition to a new economic and political system. This attitude insists that the present economic system cannot be rechanneled in the preferred direction and that its deficiencies cannot be resolved without essential changes.

The radical economic reform of the 1990s has to

address the unsolved problems of prior abortive attempts at reform and new issues surfacing in a fluctuating environment. The federal government offered its concept of changes in late 1989. The main thrust of its reform thinking and practice revolves around these interdependent goals:

- A transition to a comprehensive modern market economy

- Elimination of the predominant property rights arrangement (social ownership) and a transition to freely competing various property rights (private, cooperative, state, foreign, and mixed)

- Liberalization, deregulation, and privatization

- A transition to an open economy

- Transformation of the basic economic subjects into profit-oriented entrepreneurial enterprises

- A change in the role of the state and establishment of legal protection for the domestic and foreign interests of economic subjects

- Abrogation of political considerations in economic decisions

In previous reform attempts, the present transformation was prepared for by a set of institutional changes, new legislation, and new economic policies, these being connected with changes to the constitution under consideration by the constituent republics and federation. In the early 1990s the available options and the general framework of the transition are affected by the unresolved constitutional problems and by changes already implemented in two of the republics. The choice is between two constitutional solutions: a confederation or a federation of the republics. The solutions envisioned not only impact the institutional nature of the transition, but also affect the many details of the changes in the economic system.

This transformation of the economy requires that the behavior and function of market institutions be established. Experience has proved that in the transition from any type of command economy, introducing market institutions is easier than controlling the evolving market behavior and economic decisions.

One can foresee this new economic system cannot be implemented in a short time. This is another reason to stress the importance of the choice of transition strategy, and timing and the complementarity of institutional and policy changes.

In general, the countries in transition from a command to a market economy view the transition as a series of measures. Neither in Yugoslavia nor in the other countries in transition is there a final comprehensive blueprint for change. The transition process is therefore viewed as a succession of measures, with later steps chosen after the results of the preceding ones are known. The transition is an open-ended process in Yugoslavia, and it is expected to be lengthy. After a successful first step, the country is now entering the second transition phase, also a learning process, since no historical experience is available.

A basic issue in the choice of the transition strategy focuses on the pace of change. Countries involved in the transition must choose between a gradual versus an abrupt transition from the old system to the new.

A fast-paced strategy of transition to a market economy closes the gap quickly and includes (1) a transition from state to private property; (2) conversion of the national currency; (3) establishment of private, profit-oriented enterprises; (4) institution of commercial loans; (5) abolition of price controls; and (6) no soft budget constrains. In gradual strategy, the transition is lengthy, with strategy changes. The transition in Yugoslavia was first conceived as a gradual one, but now seems to have shifted to a fast one.

The "right" sequence of transition policies is a key ingredient to the transformation of an economy. A "best" sequence depends on what is happening in a country at the beginning, on the concept, and on the goals of the transition process.

The actual transition from a command to a market system sometimes requires painful adjustments. In the quest to establish a more viable economic and sociopolitical system, the social costs should not be overlooked when the level and distribution of losses in living standards in a given economy are chosen.

The slow transformation of the very important ownership principle during the transition process can generate considerable costs. For example, in Yugoslavia these costs impact negatively on production, and the growth of unemloyment is connected with decreasing productivity--a fall in investment activity.

The transition usually requires several phases, with the proper choice and sequence being an important consideration. In Yugoslavia there have been two distinguishable phases in the present transition. In the first phase, hyperinflation was stopped, and the halt was not accompanied by a depletion of foreign currency reserves. By 1991 internal convertibility existed, and it was expected that international convertibility under the International Monetary Fund (IMF) conditions would soon follow. The foreign debt was regularly serviced, even diminished, and Yugoslavia was no longer among the heavily indebted countries. The institutional changes during this phase met the constraints of the 1974 constitution, which goes back to the period of a "consensus economy."

In general, the stage was set for the second phase, which follows the first preparatory phase and marks the actual beginning of the transformation of the economy, a critical stage in the process. It is not possible to consider all of the problems to be solved as they relate to numerous economic, political, and social issues. Among the problems connected with complete change of the socioeconomic and political system, there looms the crucial change in the ownership structure. In Yugoslavia this is a transition from social ownership to a private, cooperative, state, and foreign ownership, a new phenomenon in content and importance. No theory is available for the solution to this problem nor to shed some light on this complicated issue, which is a general one to be met in all the countries under consideration here.

Different proposals are under consideration to change the ownership structure, from state or social ownership to private, foreign, and other. These differences are not solved and are obstacles to the transition process, for without such a change the enterprises do not respond to market signals. Among the various proposals under discussion for changes to the ownership structure are the following:

1. Privatization through sales to domestic and foreign purchasers.

2. Transformation of enterprise assets by

specific criteria into shares and distribution of the shares to employees. Such a transaction could contribute to the financial resources available for investments and promote the expansion of the capital market.

3. Transformation to state/public ownership, as a temporary solution to guarantee control over a process ripe with opportunities for graft and corruption.

4. Sales of enterprises to the workers employed in them.

There is widespread resistance to the transition in the different economies, resistance that is politically and socially motivated. The elimination of state or social property abolishes the basis for the political power of certain social groups, which therefore oppose these changes in the ownership structure. The transition to a market economy can also be opposed by those employed in state or social enterprises, because there would be less job and wage security. Bankruptcies and wage reductions also provoke dissatisfaction and conflicts in the transition process.

The transition process from any type of command to a market economy can be fast-paced but still lengthy and painful, involving the whole socioeconomic system of a country. For example, concentration on only the economic system raises many issues. All of the independent features of an economic system are intertwined in the transition to a market economy.

II

Economic Reforms

4

Political and Economic Reforms
Zivko Pregl

Government headed by President Ante Markovic assumed office in Yugoslavia on March 16, 1989. Three key reform objectives were immediately declared:

- Introduction of an integral market in Yugoslavia of goods and services--a capital market and a labor market;

- Internationalization of production and of the way of life in Yugoslavia;

- Strengthening the rule of law, the expansion of human rights in keeping with international standards, and introduction of a multiparty political democracy.

Understandably, questions have arisen as to the sequence of these moves. Should we in the government tackle political or economic changes first? Should we change the economic system first or grapple with the exceptionally high inflation? How was Yugoslavia to make these changes under conditions requiring that important decisions have the agreement of 6 + 2 + 1 factors (six republics, two autonomous provinces, and the federation)?

ECONOMIC VERSUS POLITICAL CHANGE

We decided to begin with economic changes and then proceed to the political ones. Since Markovic took office, the nature of the economic system has changed substantially. Since the end of his first year, Yugoslavia has had an economic system not unlike those of market-oriented countries. About forty laws governing the economy were amended, and many new ones were adopted. These changes to the economic system proceeded from several key principles.

The first principle accorded national treatment to aliens, with Yugoslav laws applying equally to both domestic and foreign investors. Today if a foreigner wishes to start his own enterprise in Yugoslavia, he just has to take the Law on Enterprises and stay within it; there is no special law regulating the founding of enterprises with foreign ownership in Yugoslavia.

The second principle is that of pluralism of ownership. All types of ownership are accorded equal treatment. This refers to private property, and social, state, and cooperative property, as well as the property of foreigners, which as a rule is private.

The third principle is that of the university. We made every effort to incorporate into our legislation all of the measures which have proven productive in the world, and to avoid those that have not worked. This is the reason it has been possible to found enterprises of the type found in market economies-- shareholding companies and partnerships, with rules applicable to banks.

The fourth principle is deregulation. We have substantially reduced the number of laws and provisions, to strengthen the independence and autonomy of enterprises in their entrepreneurial decisionmaking.

The fifth and last principle is symmetrical treatment of the factors of labor and capital. Under our legislation, both factors may be optimally combined to maximize profits. Understandably, the labor factor is specific, being inherent in man. But enterprises, should not be required to resolve welfare problems, which is an obligation to be undertaken by the state to free enterprises of it, so they can then channel all of their potential toward maximizing profits.

In changing the economic system, we proceeded from the values of competition, pluralism, opening toward the world, and the rule of law. This profoundly impacted the political physiognomy of Yugoslavia and made it possible to shift the focus of the government's efforts to political reforms for the succeeding year (1990-91). An opposite sequence of events, or political reforms followed by economic ones, would not have been successful.

Apart from all the criticism, we can justly make

about the past political system, and apart from the Yugoslav need for democratization and general achievements, we must admit that the changes we made have not upset political relations to the extent that they became a target for emotional attacks and opposition moves. Rather, people became more attentive to redressing the economic crisis. For those reasons we could afford the luxury, conditionally speaking, of beginning with economic reforms and thereafter proceeding to political reforms. Although this was possible at the tactical level over a short period of time, it could not have been done at the strategic level. In the strategic sense, both are very closely linked.

During the first year, economic reforms, not political ones, were initiated. The changes attracted less attention than was warranted by their comprehensiveness and depth, which was the answer to the dilemma of whether to embark first on economic or political reforms.

ECONOMIC SYSTEM CHANGES VERSUS MACROECONOMIC ADJUSTMENT

In 1988, the average inflation in Yugoslavia was at 1.5 percent, and in December 1989, prices were 2.5 percent higher than in December 1988. It is quite understandable that the government was subjected to intense pressure at the beginning of its work to proceed with measures against inflation, leaving broad changes in the economic system for a later time. Previous governments had focused their efforts on inflation without changing the economic system, but this had produced no definite anti-inflationary results. They had been able to bring about temporary lulls in price hikes, but afterwards, inflation was even stronger. This prompted the present government to change the economic system first, which was done in 1989. In December 1989 the government launched a rigorous anti-inflation program, which has produced an almost zero level of inflation. The balance of payments is sound, and foreign exchange reserves have greatly increased.

The anti-inflation program essentially consisted of two parts, one with economic policy measures and the other, the so-called heterodox shock, with psychological measures. In the first part, we introduced a very strict monetary policy, which proclaimed the dinar a convertible currency, carried out its denomination (by erasing four zeros), and pegged the dinar exchange rate to that of the deutsche mark (1 DM = 7 Din). We shifted to the fiscal area numerous tasks previously financed by money issues from the National Bank of Yugoslavia.

The essence of the psychological measures lies in the freeze on personal incomes over a six-month period. We also introduced six-month price controls over 25 percent of producer prices, primarily in the economic infrastructure. Why employ these psychological measures? There was little money in the market, so that even without a freeze on incomes, enterprises would have had a very slim chance of raising it. Also because money was scarce, the market demand was restricted, and frozen producer prices could not be increased. By putting a freeze on some categories in enterprises, we created psychological security; enterprises would not have to expect cost shocks on personal incomes and some key material inputs, such as imports, energy, and transport.

This caused the enterprises to refrain from exerting pressures for increases in their output prices. In fact, in February, March, April, and May of 1990, many enterprises reduced their prices. The price levels in Yugoslavia included a considerable reserve, which was the result of inflationary expectations. In October, November, and December of 1989, enterprises increased their prices without any calculations, simply to join the general stampede of price hikes. If income in the price structure of an interprise accounts for 25 percent, or if profit in the price structure accounts for less than 10 percent, then it could be fatal for the enterprise if it were to lag behind in the general price increase race. Therefore, in the last months of 1989, the inflation was psychologically founded, which resulted in high reserves in price levels. These reserves were exhaused because of this year's restrictive monetary policy, which explains the decrease in many prices in Yugoslavia.

The decision to change the economic system first and only then to embark on changes that would yield anti-inflationary results, was sound. The changes to the economic system created maneuvering room for enterprises when the highly restrictive monetary policy was introduced. Otherwise, the restrictive monetary policy would have led to stagnation and ruin for enterprises. Now the process of restructuring enterprises has been encouraged. The changes to the economic system and anti-inflationary measures have made it possible to initiate a new development policy. The backbone of this policy is privatization.

During the 1960s, social property, an innovation in Yugoslavia, performed its task, with the highest social product growth rates registered. Social property made it possible for workers to identify themselves with their enterprises, which explained the high growth of productivity and social product during that period, when Yugoslavia and Japan ranked at the top of the world list. Since social property has exhausted its potential for further economic and technological development, we are now currently embarking on the privatization process. This will normalize the ownership structure in enterprises, yield additional capital, and increase the efficiency of the economy. Privatization is not an end in itself; its importance is in its ability to increase the efficiency of our economy.

DECISIONMAKING IN A FEDERAL COUNTRY

Any changes of importance in Yugoslavia have to be adopted by a consensus of the republics, and the two provinces and approved by the federal bodies. The Yugoslav government was at the very outset of its work aware that nothing could be done through a philosophy of discipline or a philosophy of force; it had to offer arrangements attractive to all in the country. During the time this government has been in office, changes that no one would have dreamed possible at the beginning of 1989 have now become a reality in the economic and political systems of Yugoslavia.

The government did not strive for importance, but rather to be useful and to offer more rational solutions than those that could be implemented by any part of the country alone. The reason for Yugoslavia's existence is to solve the problems together. We must introduce an integral market; we must become international; and we must introduce multiparty democracy and strengthen the rule of law. We can do this more easily all together.

CONCLUSION

It is understandable that the steps in political democratization have raised many concerns about the organization of the Yugoslav state.

The issue of nationality relations in Yugoslavia has smouldered beneath the surface in the past, with many taboo topics now surfacing under the onslaught of democratization. The tensions existing today on the Yugoslav public scene are a normal consequence of zigzag development. After a period of uniform thinking and the monopoly of a single truth, it is now possible to openly air different views. It is natural that the process of democracy is also attended by some undesirable extreme phenomena, but that cannot deny this basic fact about Yugoslavia, namely that the process of definite democracy and a multiparty system has been initiated.

The Yugoslav government does not think that the decision to build a federation or a confederation can be made at the conference table, which is connotative of scholastic discourse. Numerous criticisms against the Yugoslav state by the nations and nationalities of Yugoslavia are rooted in negative experiences of the past. National topics, as well as related religious ones, were frequently suppressed. Numerous criticisms leveled against Yugoslavia as a whole happened when the state held the reins of economic life and carried out the predistribution of income. That is why appropriate changes should be made in the economic and political system to (1) transform Yugoslavia into a modern, economically efficient, and politically free state and (2) create conditions for discussions on the form and direction the Yugoslav state should take.

It is necessary to ensure the full equality of nations and nationalities in Yugoslavia. The sovereignty of the individual, with all the characteristics of that sovereignty, including national ones, must be protected. We must proceed from the sovereignty of nations--the sovereignty of the republics and define the functions to be discharged by the state for the interests of all. Such an approach will serve as a test for everything the state undertakes now in the redefinition of its role, and it will make opportunities for Yugoslavia to be a sound negotiator in the world arena and an attractive partner in the family of the developed countries of Europe.

5

A Supply-Side View
of the Economy
Marshall R. Colberg

I remember that a wise friend of mine did usually say, "That which is everybody's business is nobody's business."
Izaak Walton

Many American economists consider themselves to be "supply-siders," and this approach is now more popular than Keynesian "demand-side" economics. Both microeconomic and macroeconomic prescriptions can differ according to which view is taken. This chapter will examine some aspects of the Yugoslav economy from the supply side. This amounts to an application of the traditional theory of property rights, incentives, resource allocation, and competitive markets, but it is not meant to imply that demand is unimportant.

Actually, it is often difficult to separate demand and supply forces. For example, Philip H. Wicksteed and Herbert J. Davenport pioneered the concept that possessors' desires to retain their own goods can be shown in the demand curve, rather than reflecting their reservation prices in the supply curve. This view is often useful, as in analysis of the demand for money. Not selling something you own is equivalent to buying it, from an opportunity-cost point of view.

The basic problem encountered in social ownership of property is the lack of private initiative in accumulation, preservation, and operation of capital. It is not surprising that Izaak Walton, quoted at the beginning of this chapter, was impressed by this principle as he made his way along trout streams, since the trashing of land and water when individuals cannot appropriate the gains from better behavior are especially evident to the angler.

LAFFER CURVE

On the macroeconomic level, supply-side economists

are sometimes accused of believing that tax cuts pay for themselves in increased revenues to government. The Laffer curve predicts that higher tax rates bring in less revenue, but in practice this is not likely to occur. Supply-siders do, however, more correctly emphasize that the gain in revenue from a tax increase may be disappointingly small, because incentives to work and utilize capital are diminished.

OWNERSHIP AND INCENTIVES

The Yugoslav system of worker-management and profit-sharing was designed to improve morale and provide worker incentives. Although Yugoslav firms do not readily go out of business--even under adverse conditions, the workers can replace a manager--this, in effect, provides a partly new organization. Workers tend to remain with a given organization for long periods of time, and the workers often have a worthwhile stake in its accumulation of assets.

Stock Ownership

Within the general framework of the Yugoslav economy, a useful innovation would be the installation of a system of stock certificates, whereby each worker would have a definite and usually growing claim to his firm's wealth. Dividends would provide profit sharing, and the board of directors controlling financial policy would be largely made up of workers.

Some important problems would be resolved by such an innovation, including age-group conflicts, where younger workers tend to be especially interested in the long-term growth of their organizations while older workers tend to prefer more immediate income.

If stock certificates were readily saleable on the developing financial markets, individual time preferences could more readily be satisfied. Individuals desiring immediate income could sell to those who prefer long-term gains. Mobility of workers between firms would be promoted, as accumulated wealth would be portable. Stocks would constitute excellent collateral for bank loans. Investment of pension funds in dependable stocks would be facilitated. Outside ownership could be promoted to the extent desired. Some of the devices used in present day large-scale markets, such as options to buy and sell, might eventually be feasible to introduce.

Privatization

The institutional change just outlined would be an important move toward private property rights, paralleling the trend toward privatization in several European nations. The Yugoslav situation is different, however, since most of the assets that might increasingly become private, personal property are not government owned at present. Instead, they belong to the workers' organizations. A system of stock ownership could enhance privatization as "club" assets became private assets through stock ownership.

Encouragement of private enterprise, especially in fields where close contact with patrons occurs, would speed economic growth. Restaurants, hotels and motels, beauty shops, gift shops, health facilities, construction companies, and repair facilities come readily to mind and are already privately owned to some extent.

When further European economic integration occurs in 1992, Yugoslavia should vigorously attempt to take advantage of institutional changes to promote production and trade. An expanded private sector is compatible with the spirit of 1992, and joint ventures should also become more common. Tax policy toward enterprises should encourage profits derived from efficiency.

Inflation

Yugoslavia has been unable to control inflation and in 1991, it is still running at very high levels. Although a rising price level is primarily a monetary phenomenon, the supply of goods being "chased by money" is important. Supply-side policy is anti-inflationary, since its goal is to increase the availability of a large variety of goods and services. The causes of severe inflation are analyzed in other chapters.

TAXATION AND WORK

Some years ago it was popular to argue that a reduction in taxes on individuals would decrease their work effort, because they were conceived to have relatively fixed goals for wealth accumulation and the attainment of such goals was facilitated by possession of increased after-tax income. While some individuals do think this way, the more usual response to lower tax rates is an increase of work over leisure. This is all the more to be expected in the Yugoslav worker-managed firm, since retained profits belong to the workers. An innovation mentioned earlier, whereby transferable stock certificates representing equity are utilized, would strengthen the desire to save more when profits rise.

Empirical studies for the United States, as reported by Paul Craig Roberts (1989), have indicated a negative relationship between the supply of labor and the magnitude of federal and state income taxes. Probably this would hold to an even greater extent in Yugoslavia, where workers should have more power to influence the rate of output. This appears to be an important field for research.

Some indications of ownership rights can perhaps be better seen in a simple formula used in managerial economics. Letting P stand for present value of a machine or other investment good, Q for quasi-rent received at the end of each year, i for the interest rate, and S for scrap value, we have

$$P = \frac{Q1}{1 + i} + \frac{Q2}{(1+i)^2} + \frac{Q3}{(1+i)^3} + ...+ \frac{Qn}{(1+i)^n} + \frac{S}{(1+i)^n}$$

Quasi-rent, often called cash flow, is income minus total variable cost. Cash flow is implicitly assumed to be maximized each year by operations and sales that equate marginal revenue and marginal cost.

Many variables affect present value, as suggested by the formula. Quasi-rent is affected by price of output; by prices paid for labor, materials, and other inputs; and by possible breakdowns. Scrap value will depend in part on technological changes that occur during the life of the machine or other assets and the effort devoted to selling used equipment.

The interest rate to be used in discounting future income requires much information and good judgment. Usually it is correct to utilize an interest rate that reflects the market-determined rate at which the firm can lend its money, with the degree of uncertainty being the same. The desirability of curbing inflation to hold down interest rates is also evident in the formula. Once present value is estimated, comparison of P with the cost of the machine or other investment determines whether the acquisition should be made. If P exceeds the cost, it means that according to the best calculation that can be made, returns will more than cover all variable costs, depreciation, and "opportunity interest" on the capital tied up in the capital good. If cost exceeds P, the investment should not be made.

While the above view is mainly microeconomic, it can be considered more broadly as macroeconomic and important on the supply side. Factors that reduce the cost of capital equipment to the firm, such as lower interest rates, better maintenance, rises in cash flow from efficient use of labor and capital, and maximization of scrap value are all relevant to the Yugoslav economy.

SUMMARY

Since the 1930s many influential economists have been Keynesians, emphasizing that fiscal change operates to alter aggregate demand in the economy. In recent years supply side economics has gained considerable favor in academic and political circles. To some extent this is simply a renewed faith in quite traditional microeconomics, with such prescriptions as (1) lowering tax rates to encourage savings and investments, (2) encouraging more work, (3) discouraging the expenditure of time on tax returns on and developing tax shelters, and (4) improving the rate of utilization of capital.

The well-known "Laffer curve" suggests that higher tax rates may not bring in more tax revenues, or that lower rates may not decrease government revenues. Supply-side economics does not rest on this extreme position, but supply-siders do emphasize that lower tax rates tend to be partially self-supporting because they increase incentives.

Greater reliance on private property rights would stimulate the Yugoslav economy. Common ownership encounters the age-old principle that "everyone's property is no one's property." The more directly and certainly an individual can benefit from an increase in the value of an owned asset, the more interest he or she will take in promoting that rise in value.

The introduction of a system of stock certificates and development of the fledgling stock market would, in time resolve some problems presently faced by Yugoslav firms. Workers who plan to remain for a long period with a given firm are more likely to look favorably on retaining and building up its assets than are those who may soon retire or otherwise leave. Transferable stock certificates showing ownership rights would solve some of the inequities of unlike "time preferences" and would promote labor mobility. Not only would stock ownership be valuable to retired persons, but the stocks would provide excellent collateral for bank loans.

Greater deregulation, privatization, and reliance on the market to affect resource allocation would probably permit Yugoslav firms to take better advantage of the greatly increased European economic integration promised for 1992. The nations that will gain most from integration will probably be those that can quickly establish joint ventures, adjust production plans, and in general be most alert to new opportunities.

6

Prospects for Commercial Banking
Dimitrije Dimitrijevic

Financial and monetary institutions, instruments, transactions, and policies are related institutionally and economically to the "real infrastructure" of an economy. Their relationship to the institutional structure is primarily important in (1) ownership of enterprises; (2) the degree of decentralization in economic decisionmaking, especially of enterprises; (3) the roles of the goods and services, financial, foreign exchange, and labor markets; (4) the potential of these four markets for consistent valuation of goods and services (prices), valuation of financial resources (interest rates), valuation of foreign exchange resources (foreign exchange rates), and valuation of labor (wage rates); (5) the role of central and other governments in direct economic government regulation; (6) the impact of inefficient economic units (enterprises); and (7) the implementation of regulations and of penalties for abuse of regulations. The relationship to the economic structure of these institutions, instruments, transactions, and policies is primarily related to

- Level of economic development

- Regional differences in the level of economic development

- Level of productivity of labor and capital

- Sensitivity of enterprises to losses and illiquidity risks to enterprises

- Market performance and the practical ability

of markets to influence consistent valuation of goods and services, financial resources, and foreign exchange resources and labor

- Fiscal policy goals and targets

- Foreign-transaction (balance-of-payments) policy goals, targets, and measures

- Economic developments (domestic and foreign)

The real infrastructure imposes more efficient functional adjustments to the financial and monetary organization, to ensure optimal performance by the organization and by the real infrastructure and to implement policy goals and targets. The consequent interrelationships in Yugoslavia are more practical than theoretical, especially in significant changes to the real infrastructure. This requires not only a complex approach to financial adjustment problems in changes to the real infrastructure, but also the use of empirical analysis to identify relevant relationships.

In this approach, the following principles for reforming the real infrastructure of Yugoslavia deserve greater attention because of needed financial adjustments in these areas:

1. Changes in the ownership of enterprises can increase the number of private, private-social, and joint-ownership enterprises. Foreign economic units can be included as participants in the ownership of enterprises; they can also participate in ownership and management through shares, as instruments to finance the management of their capital. These changes in ownership and capital financing of enterprises are expected to motivate the enterprises to work on their goals, targets, instruments, and monetary and financial organizations.

2. Decentralization of decisionmaking should occur in the production levels and structure of enterprises in income distribution, investment, and foreign transactions (real and financial).

3. There should be more active participation by financial markets, markets in goods and services, foreign exchange, and labor, with a

concentration on the efficiency of value-pricing of goods and services, financial resources, foreign exchange resources, and labor. This should lead to greater respect for economic criteria and more rational conduct of enterprises in current transactions and in domestic and foreign investments.

4. A decrease in direct economic intervention by governments (federal, republican, provincial, and local) should occur, along with a decline in the governments' influence on economic decisionmaking by enterprises, banks, and other financial institutions. The governments' protection of these institutions in illiquidity, insolvency, and violation-of-regulations cases would be eliminated.

5. A greater respect for supply-side economic policy goals, shown in increased production and lower unemployment rates, should run parallel with anti-inflation and balance-of-payments goals and policies.

The following results of changes in the structure and function of the financial and monetary organization can be expected:

1. The structure and types of financial organizations should be radically changed. The foundation and ownership of banks and other financial organizations should be adjusted to the broader concept of ownership of enterprises, which should motivate policy changes in profit-loss motives; heighten sensitivity to risks/losses, illiquidity, and insolvency; and increase respect for banking criteria in granting credits.

2. The infrastructure of financial organizations should become adapted to the new role of financial intermediation in an environment of increased freedom in economic decisionmaking. There should be greater sensitivity to economic criteria on the part of ultimate borrowers and lenders. Financial resources (interest rates) should be consistently valued with valuation of goods and services (prices), foreign exchange resources (exchange rates), and labor (wage rates).

3. The operation of financial institutions should change because of the elimination of government influence on the decisionmaking financial institutions and the elimination of government protection of these institutions in cases of illiquidity, insolvency, and violations of regulations. It is hoped that this will lead to a greater respect for bank and market criteria in the operations of financial institutions, a greater integration of financial flows, and the elimination of the existing regional boundaries of financial flows.

4. Significant adjustments are expected in the operations of financial institutions. These will be made to accommodate financial markets and the new financial instruments used in financial markets (stocks, treasury bills, and bonds), and to adjust to the influence of supply and demand on these markets. In addition to generating respect for banking guidelines, this may contribute to the market valuation of the credits and deposits of financial institutions, which may extend the use of market interest rates and eliminate existing wide differences in the interest rates extended by banks, eliminating the practice of extending lower rates to certain groups of enterprises, which have to be covered by higher rates on credits to other borrowers.

5. The reduction in regulations on foreign financial transactions is expected to bring significant changes in the role of financial organizations in foreign lending and borrowing and also in domestic foreign exchange transactions.

6. Deregulation of payment transactions should allow banks to handle payments and all the other transactions related to the giro accounts of social enterprises and other social entities. Existing regulations allow these payments to be made only through the Social Accounting Service.

It may be concluded that these changes in the real infrastructure require radical and significant adjustments by financial organizations in goals, targets, financial policies, monetary policies, fiscal policies, and foreign financial transaction policies. Attention must be paid to the goals/targets/instruments structure of these policies and their interrelationships.

HISTORY OF REFORMS

The purpose of the following historical presentation of reforms in the financial organization is to show how it responded to radical institutional and economic changes in its real infrastructure from 1952 through 1988. The conclusions serve to reinforce the appropriateness of reforms to the financial organization and real infrastructure, in content and timing. If the adjustments by the financial organization to changes in the real infrastructure were not appropriate, the relevance of the historical inheritance to reform in 1989 and to the prospects for the future have to be reviewed.

The 1952-88 period should be reviewed, with 1952 representing the last year of centralized financial organization and the year when, contemporary financial organization reforms began. The changes in the real infrastructure (institutional and economic) will be presented first, followed by an analysis of adjustments to the financial organization and an explanation of what was needed or lacking at the end of 1988.

The basic change in the real infrastructure during this period was the decentralization of economic decisionmaking, which became the focal point of the new self-management system. This would provide greater freedom for socialist enterprises to regulate their own production, pricing, income distribution, savings, and investments. It was also expected that greater freedom in economic decisionmaking would be accompanied by more accountability of socialist enterprises for inefficient work and losses. In the financial field, this was reflected by a radical change in financing enterprises. To begin with, enterprises were to be financed by bank credits carrying the obligation of repayment of credit and interest payments, instead of nonrepayable government grants.

Parallel with this was the elimination of mandatory central planning and a decline in the government's role in economic regulations. The transfer of responsibility and decisionmaking to the governments of republics and those of the autonomous provinces or local governments represented a significant change in the role of the financial system.

The next change occurred in integration mechanisms, with (1) an increased role for free markets; (2) introduction of social agreements among enterprises and social compacts by the enterprises and governments; (3) a general nonmandatory system of social planning; and (4) indirect government economic intervention, using monetary and fiscal policy.

These changes in the role and function of the financial system are presented in the normative sense. However, the activities and implementation of the new regulations deviated significantly in the normative sense. The role of government remained very important, although it was largely transferred to the regional governments. The central government remained strongly involved in direct regulations of income distribution, prices of goods and services, interest rates, foreign exchange rates, wage rates, and foreign transactions. The republics, autonomous provinces, and local governments that were active in the implementation of regulations enjoyed a great deal of freedom to deviate from the existing regulations and strong over-normative influences on socialist enterprises and financial institutions. This was especially true in local governments, as reflected in the local triangles (local government, socialist enterprises, and banks). These involved a strong influence of local governments on the behavior of enterprises and banks, on one hand, and full protection of enterprises and banks from the results of illiquidity, insolvency, and losses, on the other.

These deviations from normative rules led to less freedom and responsibility for socialist enterprises and financial institutions. They also reflected the drastically reduced role of free markets and the inconsistencies in the economic valuation of (1) goods and services (distortion of relative prices compared with the prices on foreign markets), (2) valuation of financial resources (negative real interest rates), (3) valuation of foreign exchange resources (negative real or overvalued exchange rates on domestic currency), and (4) valuation of labor (wage rates). The excess of normative regulations and government protection of socialist enterprises, banks, and other socialist units, accompanied a lack of sensitivity to economic and market criteria and to losses/bankruptcy in current transactions and investments. In this way, the real behavior of governments, markets, socialist enterprises, banks, and other socialist units radically deviated from normative regulations.

Economic changes in the real infrastructure were significant to the structure and operation of the financial organization in the following ways:

1. The economic growth of 6 to 7 percent annual increase in real gross national product in the 1960s and 1970s meant greater respect for economic and market criteria by socialist enterprises, banks, and other economic units.

2. The greater savings and investment ratios caused more assymetric savings and investment by economic units. It also gave a more important role to financial intermediation through the stimulation of savings and rational use of financial resources, to parallel the elimination of most government/grants as instruments to finance investments.

3. Money assumed a more dynamic role in highlighting the need for appropriate monetary policy goals and instruments.

4. The increased visability of free markets imposed greater respect for economic and market criteria and made it possible to place responsibility on economic units for economic and market violations, losses, illiquidity, and insolvency.

5. Indirect economic policy measures received a heightened role in complex, nonmandatory economic planning through monetary and fiscal policy.

6. There was more freedom in real and financial foreign transactions.

In these institutional changes, however, there were significant variations from economic rules in the activities of the economic units from economic rules. The main ones came from normative and expected changes in (1) the diminuitive role of free markets for goods and services; (2) distorted markets for foreign exchange resources and no financial markets, leading to distortion of economic valuation of goods and services, financial resources, foreign exchange resources, and labor, along with logical

73

distortion in the behavior of the economic units in savings and investments, and supply and demand of financial resources; (3) the behavior of governments and economic units, which was significantly changed after the second increase in oil prices in 1979. This led to a greater respect for economic criteria in consistent economic valuation of the policy of positive interest and exchange rates, improvement of the balance of payments because of a higher inflation rate and a slowing of the rate of increase in production and unemployment. In spite of some improvements after 1979, the real infrastructure of the Yugoslav economic system remained overburdened by significant deviations from the normative economic system, especially in the over-normative role of governments, the low profile of free markets, and the economic units' lack of respect for economic and market criteria, in a climate of distorted valuation of goods, capital, foreign exchange, and labor.

The adjustments made by the financial system to changes in the real infrastructure were only partial and delayed. In 1952, the central banking system (the National Bank of Yugoslavia) was the only banking system, except for a narrow and insignificant local savings bank structure. The first steps in deentralization of the banking system began normatively in 1954, after implementation of the social self-management system. However, the real decentralization of the banking system began in 1955, when local communal banks, local cooperative savings institutions, and the Post Office Savings Bank were established with offices throughout the country. However, the central banking system remained in control of financing enterprises.

In 1961 the next step was taken on the road to decentralization of the financial system, after decentralization of economic decisionmaking and financing enterprises by changes to the real infrastructure. A new decentralized banking system was designed, to finance socialist enterprises through three types of business banks: (1) local communal banks, (2) republican business banks, and (3) federal specialized banks. The specialized banks were to finance balance-of-payments transactions, investments, and agricultural enterprises; their mission was to cover financial flows for the whole country. The National Bank of Yugoslavia was defined as a central bank, to perform only central banking operations.

Further changes were made in 1962, when payment transactions were moved from the National Bank of

Yugoslavia to a specialized institution, the Social Accounting Service. The Social Accounting Service was responsible for executing all payments through deposit money accounts, and it exercised control to ensure the legality of transactions for all social, economic, and other units.

The next step was made in 1963, when some financial operations of the federal specialized banks were transferred to republican and communal banks.

The next phase of adjustments came in 1965, parallel with reforms in the real infrastructure and in economic policy. More decentralization of the banking system was followed by the transformation of local communal banks into banks to serve the whole territory of Yugoslavia. Two types of banks were involved: commercial banks, to perform short-term operations, and banks for long-term financing, although some mixed banks performed both short-term and long-term operations. These banks, defined as regular banks, conducted their operations by international banking procedures, with the exception of the payments through deposit/money accounts of social entities, which remained within the Social Accounting Service. The founders of these regular banks were socialist enterprises, governments, and other socialist units, with no financial market institutions established.

The financial adjustment to the financial organization was made in 1974-75, by the new constitution and the banking legislation based on this constitution. The main changes occurred in the National Bank of Yugoslavia, which was now defined as a network of independent or national banks in the republics and autonomous provinces. As parts of the central banking system, these performing a dual role as regular banks for banking operations in the republics and autonomous province.

The main managing body of the central banking system was the board of governors of the National Bank of Yugoslavia. The board was composed of the governors of the national banks of the republics and autonomous provinces, and the chairman was the governor of the National Bank of Yugoslavia, with equal voting power. The national banks of the republics and autonomous provinces were made responsible for carrying out decisions made by the board of governors of the National Bank of Yugoslavia, and also to the governments of republics and autonomous provinces, which made election decisions about the governors of these banks.

The goals of the National Bank of Yugoslavia for

production, economic growth, development of prices of goods and sevices, balance-of-payments transactions, quantity of money, and volume and structure of credits were set by the federal government.

As a result, the National Bank of Yugoslavia became very decentralized in decisionmaking and in the implementation of decisions made by its board of governors. At the same time, its decisionmaking was severely limited because monetary policy goals were set by the federal government. The National Bank experienced limited involvement in (1) regulation of interest rates through its decisions about discount rates, within limits set by the federal government; (2) influence on the interest rates of banks, under conditions of no financial markets; and (3) decisionmaking in foreign transactions.

In other banks the main changes were evident. Many bank classifications were eliminated. Governments no longer influenced bank operations as founders of banks and institutions. These changes were designed to maximize the integration of financial flows and to give the institutions freedom to follow economic operations guidelines in financing investments by socialist enterprises. A money market and a foreign exchange market were established, with full control by the central banking system, but no capital market was instituted.

Activity in the economic and financial organizations during this period was very different from the way it would have been under normative regulations and expectations. Direct government regulation of economic developments in price of goods and services, interest rates, exchange rates, income distribution, and foreign transactions remained strong, and the federal government exerted powerful influence on the central banking system. The local triangles, composed of local governments, socialist enterprises, and banks shielded against illiquidity and insolvency, continued to press these institutions to depart from economic and market rules. For example, the banks were responsible for (1) neglect of banking rules, (2) regional confinement of financial flows and irrational bank credit policy, (3) neglect of repayment risks, and (4) credits given to inefficient enterprises at low interest rates. The lack of control by the central banking system was reflected in the significant departure of banking operations and social enterprises from regulations and monetary policy measures.

By the end of 1988, banking operations and the whole financial system had departed from normative regulations and economic rules to exert a significantly negative influence on the activities of socialist enterprises and the entire operation of the whole economy. This necessitated a significant change in the financial system in 1989.

PROSPECTS FOR REFORM

Any adjustments to the financial system of Yugoslavia must be made in light of the relevant institutional and economic changes and the inherited practice of past violations of normative and economic rules by financial institutions.

As the institutional and economic infrastructure changes relate to reforms in the financial system, they are important in their relationship to the following:

1. Changes in the concept and structure of ownership of socialist enterprises, using stocks as a source of capital from private owners and foreign investors. This should increase the respect of enterprises for economic criteria and for the influence of these criteria on the activities of financial institutions. Greater respect should be given to economic guidelines, and risk sensitivity to liquidity, solvency, and profitability should be heightened.

2. Further decentralization of economic decisionmaking, through reduction in the role of the federal government. It no longer exercises direct control over production, prices of goods and services, foreign transactions, income distribution, and investments. Government influence on enterprise activities and banks has been eliminated. Its protection can no longer be invoked in illiquidity and insolvency cases. These measures may increase the role of markets and economic criteria and serve to eliminate regional triangles, which are backed by the regional governments'influence on banks and enterprises.

3. Consistent valuation of goods and services, of capital, of foreign resources, and of labor, through integration of financial flows over the whole country.

4. Meaningful results from financial organization activities, through exercise of market and economic guidelines and elimination of rule violations.

5. Greater demand for efficient financial intermediation, through more savings and more prudent use of them.

6. A higher profile for monetary and fiscal policy, which should develop from these changes. This will influence decisionmaking and further the implementation of monetary policy goals, targets, and instruments.

7. A more prominent role for monetary policy in interest rate regulation. This will be a logical step because of the greater interest rate activity through market and economic strategies.

8. Deregulation of foreign financial and other foreign transactions, which should impose significant adjustments on the financial system, especially on bank operations.

These changes in the real infrastructure have required corresponding adjustment in the financial organization. However, the question of possible violations of regulations and normative rules that were inherited from the past, must be addressed. This means that the problem of reforms in the financial organization involves two basic problems: (1) how to change existing financial regulations to make them consistent with the needs of an efficiently working financial organization in the new institutional and economic environment; and (2) how to prevent financial institutions from straying from normative regulations and rules. Any new regulations must be responsive to these needs, as the financial organization makes an efficient adjustment to a new institutional and economic environment. To be responsive, the regulations must have a positive impact on the normative rules of a fully operational financial organization and must effectively eliminate rules violations.

Another area of concern related to reforms is the need for complex changes. The program of reforms in Yugoslavia involves three areas of change: the type of economic system, the role of government, and the type of political structure. Significant change must be possible in the economic and financial systems if corresponding changes are to take place in the interrelated fields. However, if direct government economic regulations and the local triangles remain, and if government's role in the elimination of violations of normative rules and regulations continues to be inefficient, a negative future will unfold.

INSTITUTIONAL CHANGES

In this aproach to reform, in 1989 institutional changes were made to the financial organization. Within the central banking system, the position of the National Bank of Yugoslavia was strengthened in control operations, although the decisionmaking mechanism did not undergo much change. The main decisions are made by the board of governors of the National Bank, but most of these decisions are made by a simple majority, instead of a two-thirds, majority. The role of the governor of the National Bank of Yugoslavia was made more important when the governor was given the option to veto decisions made by the board of governors; this veto power carries the obligation to inform the Assembly of Yugoslavia.

The National Bank of Yugoslavia shares in the interest on credits granted by the national banks of republics and autonomous provinces, as members of the central banking system (credits representing creation of reserve money), after the national banks have deducted their own costs. The National Bank share was established by new legislation, to replace the rule that the interest on these credits represented the return of the national banks of republics and autonomous provinces. The previous rule allowed the extra income from these banks to flow to republican budgets and to the governments of the autonomous provinces.

The National Bank of Yugoslavia was then empowered to exercise control over the fulfillment of legal conditions to establish banks, the adjustment of existing banks to new banking legislation, and the fulfillment of these conditions for future bank operations and other financial institutions (maximal exposure to capital investment/liquidity ratios). Crediting of the federal government by the National Bank of Yugoslavia was regulated. Only short-term credits are now permitted, to be repaid during the fiscal year to cover temporary budget deficits.

The involvement of the National Bank of Yugoslavia in the operations of money markets operations and financial markets may lead to significant changes in the instrument structure influencing the quantity of reserve money, the amount of reserve money, the amount of money in circulation, and the rates of interest and involvement in the buying and selling of government bonds.

Greater power was given to the National Bank of Yugoslavia in monetary regulations. The most important measure gave the National Bank the right to initiate and prepare proposals for laws and other decisions by the Federal Assembly in the realm of monetary policy, foreign exchange, and foreign financing. If the board of governors of the bank does not reach a decision and the governor believes that postponement of this decision may adversely affect economic development, the governor may now make decisions legally listed as decisions by the board. The National Bank of Yugoslavia gained greater freedom in its operations by being made responsible to the Federal Assembly instead of to the Federal Executive Council; however, the bank is still obligated to cooperate with the council in implementing economic policy goals.

Some basic adjustments were not made. For example, the basic decisionmaker for the central banking system has remained the board of governors of the National Bank of Yugoslavia, which, again, is composed of the governors of the national banks of the republics and autonomous provinces. The primary interest of the board members is to promote the interests of their own republics and autonomous provinces, instead of the whole economy. In addition, the National Bank of Yugoslavia remains unable to implement monetary policy measures directly. This means that the implementation of these measures remains in the hands of the banks of the republics and autonomous provinces. If the board of governors were instead transformed into a macroeconomically oriented board of experts, the board would be better able to assist the governor of the National Bank and would make him more fully responsible for the bank's decisions.

Presumably these infrastructural institutional and economic changes will allow further changes in the central banking system, emphasizing greater freedom in economic decisionmaking and a more differentiated financial organizational structure. It would improve the financial instruments in market operations. Practical experience may encourage a more radical approach, with clear emphasis on the role and make-up of the board of governors of the National Bank of

Yugoslavia and on the power of the bank's governor in monetary policy.

Significant legislative changes were made in other financial institutions. The ownership of business banks, the most typical financial institutions outside the central banking system, underwent radical change. Stocks were made the source of capital of these banks, which are owned by both socialist and private entities (domestic and foreign). This type of ownership, and the new concept of the business bank as a profit-minded institution, is expected to bring greater respect for market and economic standards in losses, illiquidity, and insolvency risks, with a more careful analysis of the creditworthiness of borrowers.

After a financial institution is created by socialist entities, socialist enterprises, or governments, then private parties (domestic or foreign) may become stockholders and participate in the decisionmaking process with the original founders and shareholders. The 1989 regulations imposed several rules designed to guarantee the proper behavior of financial institutions the following:

1. A minimal capital fund of 20 million dinars, or the maximal amount of investments based on the capital of financial institutions of twenty times more than the amount of the capital of the financial institution.

2. Maximal exposure of financial institutions to finance individual borrowers.

3. The term structure investment related to the resources or liabilities of the financial institution and the minimal liquidity ratio or holding of reserve money with the central banking system.

4. A broader role for the central banking system in controlling the implementation of these rules, along with the right of the system to discontinue the existence of a financial institution not following these rules. This includes the right not to allow further existence and transformation of existing financial institutions not satisfying these rules at the end of the legislatively determined period of late 1989. In this way, the National Bank of Yugoslavia's document confirms that the bank will fulfill the legal

rules. The document sets the essential preconditions for founding a new bank and circumscribes its future operations. The existing financial institutions are to be into organizations in compliance with new banking legislation.

The top management body of the bank is its assembly, which decides on the foundation of the bank, on its financial organization, and on its basic banking operations, including banking bylaw decisions. The execution of assembly decisions rests with the executive board and bank manager--both appointed by the bank assembly. The bank manager, who is appointed by the bank assembly, is responsible for implementing decisions made by the assembly and the executive board. He represents the bank, organizes its operations, and shoulders the responsibility for its operations'legality. The supervisory committee, which is appointed by the assembly, is responsible for supervision of all bank operations, including those of the executive board and the manager. The bank may establish a loan committee, to implement decisions in crediting bank customers; other bodies may also be instituted to facilitate bank operations.

Bank and other financial organizations are charged to cooperate with other banks (compound banks, joint banks, and bank consortiums). A special type of bank represents "mixed owners," including domestic or foreign entities.

Basically, the mission of these 1989 bank regulations is to protect the interests of bank customers. The new legislation has granted the banks and other financial organizations broader freedoms in their practical operations, organization, cooperative ventures in foreign transactions, and ties with foreign financial organizations.

The other financial organizations, as defined in the new legislation, are the Postal Savings Institution, regular savings banks, other savings organizations, and other financial organizations.

Along with banks and other financial organizations, the new legislation establishes financial markets through money markets, capital markets, and foreign exchange markets. These are expected to add to the efficiency and differentiation in financial flows and bank operations. Legislation on securities supports these developments and defines the types of securities (shares, bonds, treasury bills, certificates of deposits, and commercial notes) and operations with securities.

These normative changes in financial organizations are considered consistent with the changes in the economic system and the role of the financial organizations. In an expanding climate of market activity, the changes that have taken place in these areas have generated more respect for the accompanying economic criteria. It is logical to analyze the economic climate surrounding full implementation of the normative rules and regulations and the reasons for any significant departure from standard procedures by financial institutions.

Implementation of the new normative financial organization and its operation is closely linked to implementation of economic, governmental, and political reforms. The crucial question is whether the federal government is ready to discontinue or minimize its policy of direct economic intervention. The regional governments would eliminate the triangle of influence and paternalism by which local governments protect and finance inept local enterprises, finance irresponsible local investments, and confine financial flows within their own regions.

The problem that local and other regional governments have to face is the assumption that a large number of inept enterprises are protected within the framework of their financing. If so, a consistent and normative approach could signal the demise of these enterprises and a sharp increase in unemployment and social problems. In addition, a normative approach to financing enterprises would involve the need to eliminate extra employment, and increase the labor productivity of the enterprises and require them to follow market and economic guidelines. If the regional governments remain responsible for economic and social development, it is doubtful that they will permit strict implementation of the regular rules of social enterprise financing, regardless of the effects of applying the normative rules of financing to eliminate the existing nonproductive enterprises, low labor productivity, and low capital productivity.

Since government plays a role in political reform, if political reform is postponed, elimination of the government role in, and responsibility for, economic and social development is likely to be postponed as well. This could mean delaying full implementation of financial organization reforms in the environment. Experience with the impact of the government role prior to 1989 reveals that violations of the normative rules of this reformed financial organization should not be excluded as the results of partial (noncomplex) reforms in causally interrelated fields.

Another set of problems in the full implementation of the new, normatively defined financial organization arises in the business banks, through the high investment-to-capital ratios of business banks and the high visibility of their credits to individual enterprises. New regulations limit bank investments of twenty times more than the amount of the capital of the enterprise. In many cases, this ratio is greater than 20 percent, which decreases bank investments in credits to socialist enterprises.

Also, if the current regional confinement of financial flows is not eliminated soon, a negative backlash may cause enterprises to finance flows at a lower level of efficiency. In addition, the business banks continue to issue large amounts of credit to enterprises, in excess of the maximum ratio allowed under the new regulations. This is noticeable in regions with one or two large socialist enterprises as the main employers. The business banks are the main source of incomes for these regions, and they hold sole borrowing potential from the regional bank because of the regional confinement of financial flows.

Should the existing local banks become financial institutions? They would have to operate under regular bank rules as profit-minded institutions, governed by private and foreign shareholders, and the adhere to the regular bank rules for profit, liquidity, and solvency.

Governments may also be founders of banks. Being aware of what happens when bank rules operate with less efficient regional enterprises, the governments might be reluctant to involve their shareholders and might insist on implementing bank rules in bank operations to find a way to prevent, or at least deter these entities from becoming shareholders of bank capital and participants in bank management. If the governments continue in their economic development role, with responsibility for regional, economic, and social development, they will insist on a continuation of present banking behavior or neglect of bank rules to finance socialist enterprises, in spite of the normative rules requiring respect for the banking and economic rules of profitability, liquidity, and solvency.

In establishing financial markets by new legislation, money market and other financial markets can be established to play a significant role in financing. However, there are many operational difficulties in these markets, since their function is tightly interwoven with the function of other financial institutions, especially business banks. As a result, problems arising from the regular function of banks may impact negatively on financial market operations. Along with this, the Yugoslav economy is at a relatively low level of economic development, and financial markets play a significant role in financing in developed economies, with a higher level of differentiation in the supply and demand of financial instruments. This may be very important in Yugoslavia if the lack of experience and tradition are considered. Healthy financial markets require lively interest on the part of potential participants, although this kind of attentiveness is less important for money markets and foreign exchange because of the role of the central bank in these markets. However, capital market operations require nurturing by other financial organizations, banks, and governments.

CONCLUSIONS

The trials and tribulations of the reform process in the financial system suggest two basic conclusions:

1. Implementation of new legislation dealing with the financial system requires relevant economic, government, and political reforms.

2. The timing of these reforms must be considered, since it is difficult to implement all of the reforms immediately. Optimal timing, with financial reforms as with others, is an integral, but elusive, part of the process. Since all of these reforms cannot be implemented immediately, several stages should be planned. However, the question arises as to the content of the reforms in the subsequent phases and the content of the reforms to the financial system in these phases. The reforms made in 1989 and 1990 herald a very important phase in the reform process in financial organization.

The prospects of a real adjustment of the financial organization and its operations within a normatively defined set of rules depend on the complex involvement of causally interrelated reforms in the political system, in government economic intervention, and in the entire economic system. The prospects of an adjustment also depend on the timing of these reforms and changes in the reform process.

7

Federalism: The Crossroads
Ivo Fabinc

In Yugoslavia's history the problems associated with federalism are closely linked to difficulties in finding the right way to live together in a highly diverse geopolitical space, only recently politically integrated. These problems may be divided into two phases: one from 1918 to 1945, and the other since 1945.

Over the past two decades, Yugoslavia has undergone a drastic reexamination of its federal system, which was constructed during the war of liberation, when the mood of the country was quite different. The important changes introduced in the 1974 constitution and the last amendments to it were not sufficient to soften the impending social crisis. Yugoslavia had reached neither a desirable level of social amalgamation nor a necessary perception of the advantages to cooperative living. Not only is it unrealistic to envision Yugoslavia as a melting pot in the foreseeable future, but it is dangerous as well.

As a starting point for any change, we must accept the existence of a specific world of nations, nationalities, religions, and the six republics, which are linked together formally in a federal state but coexist under the rather strange rules of the 1974 constitution. For many neutral observers, this document expressed a nascent confederalism.

This constitutional inconsistency resulted from two conflicting long-term processes.

On the one hand, an intensive decentralization of the highly concentrated federal/state functions was underway, paralleled by the growing autonomy of the economic system, in a process unique to Eastern Europe, leading to the successful launching of industralization in an underdeveloped country.

At the same time, the pressing problems of unequal regional development, poor economic performance, and financial instability reinforced state interventionism at all levels--central, republican, and local. Although the state monopoly in foreign trade had already been abolished in 1952, the state continued to intervene in foreign economic policy. In general, the influence of the republics in shaping and implementing foreign policy was negligible.

The hidden reality of these controversial tendencies was the ideological mistrust of the state bureaucracy. This mistrust was present in the concept of an integral self-management system, which never overcame the dominant distribution function of the state. In a country with strong north-south contrasts and wide differences in the effectiveness of the economic players' ability to play the game, the "rent-seeking" effect determined the behavior of influential clusters of interests and governmental institutions. Once the indisputably charismatic influence of Marshal Tito vanished and the importance of other integrative factors successively diminished, a struggle for political power and control over state machinery erupted. The federal decisionmaking system was weakened, and the never-extinguished nationally oriented political forces in the republics reappeared to support major changes, not only to the federal system but in political, social, and economic life.

There are no simple solutions to Yugoslav problems. The complex function of such a disaggregated, large system warns us not to underestimate the transformation problems of the Yugoslav federation. From this point of view, the purely juridical alternative of federation or confederation is misleading in a certain sense.

The fundamental necessity is to have a clear insight into the environmental conditions that would nurture a new type of social contract, a modernized Rousseau-esque scenario, that could be accepted and implemented by all constituent parts or republics for a Yugoslavia of the future.

The choice of a contractarian approach has the advantage of avoiding determinative (yes or no) voting. It opens up dialogue on an interrepublican level, which should lead to an understanding of what the real problems are. Consequently, an efficient nonmarket decisionmaking process, determining the architecture of a democratic sociopolitical order in a market-oriented society, will have a better chance of being established.

By accepting the contractarian approach, we implicitly decide on dialogue rather than confrontation. Stressing the importance of a dialogue process, we also highlight the importance of good timing and well-chosen actions if we are to reach a desirable result through a community of the Yugoslav republics.

A DIALOGUE-AND-CONTRACT APPROACH: THE NORMS

On the interrepublican level, the ideal dialogue and actions would be strongly opposed to any form of domination. No effective social contract is possible if it is based only on selfish utilitarianism. Therefore, the commonly accepted rules of dialogue are a precondition for achieving a necessary degree of fairness in the negotiating process. In this context it is well to remember the words of James M. Buchanan, the 1986 winner of the Nobel prize in economics, when he warns us about the three demons that plague the conventional way of applying economics, namely the utilitarian calculus, the urge toward social engineering, and the elite mentality.

The influence of the last two demons is already limited, thanks to a deeper insight into the function of social systems in an interdependent world. However, the utilitarian calculus needs further consideration.

The rationale of a demons syndrome is certainly not to stress once more the well-known difficulty of deriving the welfare functions of the Bergson-Samuelsons type from individual utilities preferences, through majority voting or through any other aggregate procedure. Instead, the rationale is to represent the preferences of a collectivity and to satisfy the Pareto optimum criterion as the only accepted value criterion. The arrows impossibility theorem and the impossibility of a Paretian liberal are the relevant arguments. The arrows are directed primarily against allowing a pervasive worldwide bureaucracy or allowing the state to assume Leviathan proportions; they are not directed against the state as such.

The necessity is acknowledged of implementing a number of general and specific functions already known from the venerable neoclassical tradition, such as the presence of public goods, externalities, the lack of competition, social interventionism, and large infrastructural systems.

Indeed, what we are really searching for is protection of the citizen and of the whole social structure against the voluntarism of rulers commanding the state insitutions, thereby increasing the effectiveness of the global social system. The analogy between the individual and the state, and consequently the organic theory of the state, is inappropriate. The analogy between a state and the market appears more appropriate, assuming that both have to reveal consumer or voter preferences if they are to function as pillars of a market economy and a democratic society.

Having a wide knowledge of the disfunctions of the market, we have yet to accept that there is no ideal state, no ideal democracy, and no ideal voter. We have to complete the classical and popular understanding of democracy with a mechanism for public or social choice in a complex, nonmarket process of decisionmaking for public or social goods. In Yugoslavia, which has an interrepublican contract, a new mechanism for common goods choice is being introduced as a constituent part of the common welfare of the contracting parties.

In this approach the utility criterion as such is certainly not discarded, but both autonomous state utility and a populistic concept of utility are superseded. What really matters is a qualification or redefinition of utility that reflects the larger problem of a contemporary concept of rationality.

Aristotle's concept of the "social animal" is not sufficient to explain the limits of purely rationalistic selfish behavior. The theory of games-- especially the "prisoners' dilemma"--brings us nearer to an understanding of the advantage of cooperative behavior, which is largely proved by the numerous nonoptimal results of uncooperative behavior.

For an efficient dialogue among the republics, these modified utility and rational concepts are needed to obtain from the new social contract a higher common welfare than can be derived from the Hobbesian "homo hominis lupus" alternative or from the "status quo" solution. In other words, certain preconditions must exist to enable the contracting parties to engage in an efficient dialogue.

One would expect that the contracting parties could cancel the normative, even utopian visions they and their relatives have of political and social life. But if the contracting parties insist on their rigid initial positions, expecting changes in the initial positions of their partners or opponents, then this could be the beginning of a civil war or revolution. Such an attitude would certainly neither entertain a dialogue, nor promote a consensus, nor even permit what is known in the political world as compromise. A more pragmatic approach is necessary, though not always popular in a tense and deeply disturbed social life such as the present one in Yugoslavia. But until political change for dialogue exists, the validity of a widely accepted and confirmed political wisdom remains untouched.

The contractarian approach, which is different from the traditional social welfare function treatment, focuses our attention on the process of collective decisionmaking. As a starting point, the original position of hypothetical equality of the contracting parties, like the John Rawls (1971) or John Harsanyi (1975) initial impartiality position, selects certain basic principles of a fair dialogue. No dialogue can even start if the contracting parties are not able to assure these conditions.

This does not mean that we ignore the existing inequalities of the contracting parties. It is only through these negotiations that a common basis for their correction can be found, which can enhance the possibility of meaningful dialogue.

We should not accept this approach as a social panacea for all the evils of modern society; however, we can certainly find in the two principles of Rawls (1971) or in the ethical preferences of Harsanyi (1975) in the practice of international organization, or in similar approaches, new arguments for cooperation and against a simplistic rationality. We can consider these principles to be a beginning for any kind of social contract of a modern, constitutional character.

The mastery of a dialogue to obtain the expected common results is an expression of a high degree of political culture. The world is in search of a new concept, solidarity, and common progress through dialogue and mutual understanding--also a need shared by the Yugoslav republics.

We could express the idea of the initial impartial status of the republics in a common declaration of their independent sovereignty republics and their intention to progress to an interrepublican agreement about the transformation of the present constitutional system.

The main goal of this declaration would be to avoid any possible position of dominance, giving to all republics the same starting position and opening the way to frank, constructive, and efficient dialogue on all of the issues of a second common interrepublican document of a constitutional character. This might tentatively be called an agreement on the constitution of a community of Yugoslav republics.

At this stage the external position of Yugoslavia need not be changed. Notification of the declaration and of the forthcoming activities should be sufficient to allow an imperturbable transition to a community of Yugoslav republics. There is also no need to make any changes in the present interrepublican borders or place any obstacles impeding the flow and free movement of goods, capital, and population in Yugoslavia.

The possible principles of (1) a fair dialogue of equal rights to liberty and opportunity, (2) maximization of the welfare of the neediest, and (3) willingness to understand the preferences of others, are different from a set of common "goods" to be made known in an interrepublican arrangement.

Not all of these goods have to be rediscovered in an enlightened mood. A number of them are already a part of worldwide accepted values, or already closely associated with the special needs of survival or development.

INTERREPUBLICAN ARRANGEMENT AND EXTERNALLY DETERMINED COMMON GOODS

One of the most limiting influences on the selfish behavior of the countries and their institutions is the highly interdependent world as a composite system, linking together the elements of the economic, social, and cultural life in an insoluble manner. Every day we are more aware of a common destiny, although we still have to confront the permanent challenges of an irrational, self-destructive way of life.

In the postwar world community and for the first time in history, interest in cooperative behavior has been expressed through a number of universal or regional institutions, declarations, and conferences. A wide spectrum of common goods is defined for their members, subscribers, or participants, covering almost all of the fields of human activity.

For our purpose, we introduce three groups of arrangements or contracts among the states. The first group expresses the common good in the concepts and procedures that implement a number of rules or postulates of a constitutional nature on fundamental human rights; equal legal treatment of nations, religions, and races; and the rights and duties of the states in their dealings with each other and relationships with their citizens. For member states, these rules are an admonition; they define the borders of civilized behavior. They are a legal protection for citizens against the misuse of state power. For the world at large, they are more than wishful thinking about living in peace and dignity. Good examples of the first group are the UN charter and the Helsinki accord.

The second group of arrangements expresses the common good in the concept and the procedure of implementation of a code of norms about the intercommunication among member states in different fields. For the member-states this code represents an external regulatory mechanism for their foreign relations. Good examples of the second group are international economic organizations, like GATT and IMF, or regional organizations, like OECD.

The third group of arrangements expresses the common good in the programs and implementation procedures of the spatial, functional, and institutional integration process of independent states in a new community of countries. For the members, this process represents a broad new degree of activity within an enclosed socioeconomic space. A good example of the third group is the European Community.

The universal and regional common good applies to the Yugoslavia of today, too. Conceived common goods can be accepted as an integral part of the republican constitutions and the interrepublican arrangement. Through this approach, a great deal of confusion, superfluous burdening of party programs, parliamentary activities, and above all voluntarism can be avoided.

The participation of any state in a number of world or regional organizations and activities on a voluntary basis does not limit but rather broadens its potential for a higher level of social welfare for its citizens. The ultimate test of the progressiveness of any society and its institutions is the openness toward new forms of cooperation and toward the larger processes of world or regional integration, when these processes operate under fair conditions. This is in full conformity with a correct understanding of social utility and a will to participate in ameliorating the world system, conceived as a common good of the highest human value.

EUROPEAN INTEGRATION PROCESSES: A REFERENCE MODEL--POSSIBILITIES AND LIMITS

For a large number of European states, the integration process is a high-priority item, regarded as necessary for the common good of all. However, in Yugoslavia the processes are not moving in the opposite direction. Since the federal government has developed a solid network of interaction with Europe, the question is whether this European experience can serve as a model for our country.

It is not necessary to repeat all of the steps of more than three decades of West European integration and to annul the advantages of having an already open and large transrepublican market, of great value not only for the entire Yugoslav economy but also for its foreign partners, especially foreign investors. To deploy an army of customs officers and policemen on all interrepublican borders, forming a new border infrastructure and introducing a system of foreign economic instruments and policies, would appear to other Europeans as an act of economic suicide. Instead, the republics could therefore exploit the advantages of the existing system and improve their transrepublican economic relations, guided by the experiences of the EC program. They should try to complete their internal market by 1992, to make it possible to come under the European Single Act. This would not only be a new common good to be conceived and successively implemented, but also a way to a better understanding of the new rationalities of the European and world economies.

The European experiences, as well as those of all developed countries, could serve as models of economic behavior and efficient organization. Yugoslavia's main problem focuses on how to include all its parts in a large and expanding European Market and world economic community.

This path leads to adaptation problems as the Yugoslav economy tries to adjust to the new exigencies of the world economy, especially the European aspect of it. There is no way that any of the republics can bypass this difficult transition period on their way to a new economics.

At the core of the actual problem is the ability to open the economy and society to respond to the challenges of the environment, which means to create a climate of global competitiveness for the economic players and a political compatibility with the "rules of the game" that will be acceptable to the international community. This will be the final goal of economic and political reforms in any kind of common solution to everyday struggles.

In this context the long-term active role of Yugoslavia, with its comprehensive arrangements with the EC and the European Free Trade Association (EFTA), is a precious capital not to be wasted. These represent a dynamically conceived common good in an interrepublican contract; there is no better channel to meet the new and existing needs of all levels of society and all the republics, not only in their interstatal relations but in Europe and the world structure.

Undoubtedly, the EC institutions, from the Treaty of Rome forward, were especially inspired by the contractarian approach, being determined by a commonly chosen transfer of functions from the individual to the community level. In the successive degrees of integration, the alternative between federalism and confederalism never appeared, because this old legalistic approach was surpassed by fresh ideas of important theoretical and practical value for integration mechanisms.

Taking this historical evolution of the EC as a model does not mean copying its institutional solutions and transferring them to the new interrepublican arrangement; differences in the starting positions of the contracting parties must be taken into account. The main difference is that the sovereign European countries that are members of the EC were building their institutions in a process and spirit of growing integration, while in Yugoslavia, the old federal institutions were dissolving. However, certain messages from the institutional architecture of the EC can still serve as guides for questions that will arise during the drafting of the interrepublican arrangement.

It is perfectly clear that changes in the federal system alone will not be an effective solution to the Yugoslav social crisis. It is also evident that without a new social contract, the transformation of the Yugoslav economy and the republican economies cannot be achieved.

CONTENT AND FUNCTION OF THE NEW SOCIAL CONTRACT

The content of the interrepublican agreement should respond to the common needs of the contracting parties and provide for the efficient function of the system as a whole in a cooperative effort, rather than encourage civil war or an anarchic alternative.

This will necessitate a specific nonmarket decisionmaking process, based on fair dialogue and the spirit of a rationally modified concept.

The central point is that the interrepublican arrangement must not simply be a reproduction of the republican constitutions, although it will have to be based on them. The relation is not a hierarchical one; the difference is qualitative. The contracting parties are not the same, and the contents of the social contracts must differ. The interrepublican arrangement is not to be conceived of as a common constitution, although it has a constitutional character. When combined with the republican constitutions, it will represent a global constitutional system of the community of republics.

The starting position will be determined by (1) a common declaration of independence by all of the republics, (2) a realistic appreciation of the advantages of a common internal market, and (3) preservation of the already assured status in the European and world environment. The interrepublican arrangement has to contain a set of explicit external and internal common goods and the mechanisms to implement them.

I have already analyzed the categories of external goods for substantial inclusion in the arrangement. For internal common goods, the arrangement should definitely affirm (1) the creative individual initiative, (2) the constitutional position and the limits of state power, and (3) the crucial role of a broad network of economic, social, and political groups in a market oriented and democratic society, if the future holds restraint for the bureaucratic octopus.

The interrepublican arrangement would be a document of political and ethical significance, to moderate the natural preponderance of economic and developmental questions. Yugoslavia has already had a lot of good and bad experiences, and is now able to critically filter methods to maintain a concerted level of political cooperation and function.

The traditional belief was the country's economy can be managed in an autonomous, independent manner, through state interventionism in interaction with a closed internal market. This belief has been superseded and has to be replaced by a larger vision of a self-regulating system of economic participants, with the state functioning on all levels to the agreed and changing tasks. In addition, a wide range of external influences by instruments of economic policies of other countries in an open economy must be be taken into account. Therefore, a flexible coordinating mechanism on the new community level is necessary for both political and economic issues of common interest.

It is an accepted principle that common institutions should be based not on an abstract scheme, but on mutually acceptable, specific economic, social, and political practices that can, when necessary, be adapted to changing events. When alternatives appear, a careful "cost and benefit" analysis should be used to help select rational solutions acceptable to all contracting parties. If those in control have to present the results of chosen alternatives to their electorates to win their approval, those in control will be less likely to indulge in euphoric behavior.

Differences can be taken into account, but the subsequent stages in the political process of decisionmaking--the constitutional stage, the parliamentary stage, and the administrative and judicial stage--must be preserved.

From this view, the institution of the ministerial council, organized and convened to deal with emerging problems, could assure the necessary coordination--flexible and efficient--through ministerial resolutions, to be approved through relevant procedures. A common commission or similar institution could implement ministerial resolutions and serve as a qualified sponsor of activities and programs of common interest.

Two independent institutions of a general character, a council of the republics and an assembly of the republics could be introduced. The council should be oriented to the general, common questions of civil rights--individual, national, and religious liberty--and any other issues of personal conviction and actions, such as general questions about cultural welfare in a broad transnational framework. The assembly should carry out legislative activities of common interest, including the completion and renovation of the political and economic systems, and coordination of the different systemic solutions on a republican level.

To best reveal the political preferences of the electorate, two different electoral and voting procedures should be used: The first at the citizen level, and the second at the republican level.

The enlarged slogan, "Europe and the world to the European," has the same appeal as the ideal of an international community and Europe as a community of effective sovereign states, free nations, respected nationalities, and honored ethnic groups. No artificial borders are acceptable for our citizens, and this should be visible in the institutional structure of the new community.

Instead of a harsh polarization on the question of military organization, a feasible long-term program to reduce the military forces should be launched, with a historical beginning to dismantle the old military blocs. The necessity of merging the whole military organization and its related activities with new realities is already widely accepted. Nothing should be undertaken that could lead to sudden and unforeseen dramatic changes in the security of the single republics or the new community.

A distinction has to be made between the ambitions of the republics as sovereign states on the international scene, on the one hand, complex and expensive federal organization of foreign services and the presence of the community of republics in the activities of numerous international and regional organizations, on the other hand. A compromise is necessary, because it is in the interest of each republic, and of the whole country, to cover, as agreed on, the totality of the world scene. This has to be done for political reasons, and for the protection and support of the economic players. There is no need to disturb the whole network of diplomatic motions or to precipitously sever existing relations with the world.

In accepting the world community's rules of behavior, the republics cannot be conceived of as entities unto themselves, with a license for double-dealing or for neglecting the internal national, religious, and political rights and preferences of their citizens, and of their multidimensional and multi spatial organizations or regions. The logic of the dialogue and the modified principle of utility and rationality cannot be blocked on the republican borders, and arbitration procedures must work on a daily basis.

SUMMARY

History will reveal whether a community of republics in Yugoslavia is feasible, based on the principles outlined. The unpredictability and volatile nature of the scenarios in these areas is legendary. Attempting to settle these differences through violent nationalism and populism is no less dangerous to the fragile buds of an emerging democracy than it would be to neglect the national or regional controversies or regress to archaic solutions. It is unanimously agreed that the separation alternative should be constantly open to all.

It is also true that the peoples of Yugoslavia have accumulated a wealth of wisdom through their tragic history. It is therefore possible that we are in the presence not of an end, but of the beginning of a revitalization of the ideal of living together on quite different grounds.

8

The Business Institution: An Instrument of Reform

Dan Voich, Jr., and E. Ray Solomon

The shifts in socioeconomic and political initiatives that are occurring throughout the world emphasize the need to reassess the way in which the business institution provides for the economic needs and wants of society, yet satisfies people's various social values and priorities. This chapter explores the role of the business institution and business education as instruments of socioeconomic and political reform.

The first part of this chapter reviews some important historical events evolving since the industrial revolution and shows how they have influenced the management of organizations and the development of formal business education programs. This discussion focuses on the experiences of the Western world.

The second part discusses culture, business, and management in transition within the framework of current management theory and business practice.

The third part examines some specific issues relating to this transition and explains how business practice and education are affected as socioeconomic and political systems change.

HISTORICAL ANTECEDENTS

The emergence of the business institution and the

Parts of this paper are adapted, with permission from Dan Voich, Jr., and E. Ray Solomon, from their unpublished manuscript, Culture, Business and Management.

formal development of business education as a separate discipline had important roots in the cultural rebirth from 1500 to 1700. This period gave rise to several major socioeconomic and political ideas, which not only served as critical preconditions for the emergence and growth of the Industrial Revolution, but remain important elements of modern business practice and education.

One of these ideas, the Protestant ethic, emerged as a social force founded on the spirit of self-reliance and the social sanction of work. This led to the rise in achievement motivation, acceptance of the work ethic, and acknowledgment of business as an honorable profession. According to the Protestant ethic, people who are productive in the sense of work will be satisfied both economically and socially. The Protestant ethic embodies a form of social Darwinism; it supports the notion of survival of the fittest. Thus, entrepreneurship, innovation, and self-reliance became important goals for society. These goals were initially transmitted to people initially through family enterprises and later through various formal types of trade and university business education programs, as well as business enterprises.

The market ethic is a second major force produced by the cultural rebirth. This ethic is an assumption that productivity is maximized through economic freedom. The spirit of entrepreneurship, combined with economic freedom, should breed innovation and discovery, which should benefit not only the individual entrepreneurs, but society as a whole. Therefore, science and reason would be applied effectively to resolve economic problems, and this would eventually improve the social and cultural fabric of society. Also, the technological and economic innovations would be made that are necessary to permit a large accumulation of resources. This would further expand the production systems, to provide more and better goods and services to society. As the shift from a state-controlled economy to a market-directed economy was made, merchantilism evolved into capitalism. Trade began to expand through economic competition and innovation. This expansion was followed by growth in individual prosperity and the development of a middle class in society.

The third major idea produced by the cultural rebirth is the liberty ethic, which it presumed that productivity could be enhanced through individual and political freedom and laissez faire economic policy.

The liberty ethic produced the Age of Enlightenment, wherein private property rights, contracts, the right to profits, constitutional government, and human rights became important working doctrines for business institutions as well as for individuals. Reliance on these doctrines was to permit individuals and business enterprises to develop to their fullest potential, thereby providing maximum benefits to society. The liberty ethic advocated a political system based, not on the dictates of the few, but on law, equality and justice within a framework of political freedom and laissez-faire economic policy. Essentially, the liberty ethic provided social endorsement of the Protestant and market ethics, through laws and government, which enabled the Protestant and market ethics to develop and grow to their fullest potential.

These three ideas produced by cultural rebirth created an environment supportive of the emergence and development of the industrial revolution and the spirit of capitalism. As the industrial revolution grew and expanded, its implications for the development of business and management theory were broad. The large accumulation of resources by business firms made them capital intensive, and new ways of financing large enterprises were needed. The large capital investments created hidden costs and the need for more effective management of risk. New planning and forecasting techniques were needed, not only to span considerably longer periods of time, but to consider the risk and probability of losses as well as gains.

Since larger organization in turn required more employees, this resulted in greater division and specialization of labor and more extensive systems to delegate authority and decentralize operations. These large and more formal systems of organization and management and their use of greater authority created the need to study organizational arrangements and management processes that were very different from those needed for the smaller, family-controlled enterprises. A greater and more diverse number of people became concentrated in large business enterprises. Different kinds of incentives for labor had to be developed to ensure a steady supply of qualified employees and managers. Also, the number of managers needed greatly exceeded the number that could be acquired solely from the family of a business owner which created a need for more business and management education programs.

These developments during the industrial revolution

and the age of enterprise led to the recognition that the job of manager within large, complex business organizations had to be defined so that the practice of business and management could be studied and taught. Initially, this study focused on technical and manual work systems at the lower levels of the production organization, to improve efficiency in the workplace. Later, with the emergence of mass production techniques and assembly lines, attention was focused on process management, automation of work, and the job of middle- and upper-level managers.

The large growth in production systems necessitated new types of distribution channels, and eventually marketing systems, to reach and develop geographically distant markets. Changes in production scheduling, inventory control, and plant locations reflected this need. With this high degree of geographic dispersion and integration of markets, the development of individual marketing concepts evolved into formal marketing theory.

With these changes in production and marketing, other functional areas of business formally evolved and developed. Accounting, finance, purchasing, inventory control, personnel, risk management, and other specialized areas grew in importance. These specialized areas were needed to improve the planning, allocation, and control of major resources in the firm, such as men, materials, money, and machines, within the context of large-scale production and marketing systems. The large capital requirements of these systems created a need for new financial management concepts. As these concepts evolved, theories of corporation finance, investments, and financial institutions emerged.

Colleges of business were instrumental in formalizing concepts and techniques in each of these functional areas, and they developed curricula tailored to the needs of business firms. In many cases these colleges were instrumental in changing the ways business firms performed various functions, made financial decisions, controlled operations, organized their employees, and integrated their overall operations.

The large growth in the formal structure and size of business organizations also created social and psychological problems in the workplace. Informal organizations, interest groups, and differing sets of personal and social values in the workplace were identified and recognized as being significant variables to be considered in using more formal, authority-based management concepts. Eventually theories of organization behavior, motivation, and leadership evolved, drawing on concepts from psychology and sociology. These behavioral concepts became highly integrated in the curricula of colleges of business during the latter half of the twentieth century, and they are used extensively in modern business organizations.

As the institution of business grew and prospered during the late nineteenth and early twentieth centuries, the large accumulation and exploitation of resources also created serious public concerns. Frontiers began to disappear; labor became exploited; and vast power became centralized in the few. Interest shifted from exploitation of resources to rationalization of resources, and greater concern was given to the equitable distribution of the income of the firm and of the wealth of society. These concerns broadened to include the need to conserve resources, limit growth, and provide protection for the environment.

The Great Depression of the 1930s drastically diminished the unqualified support of the Protestant, market, and liberty ethics as necessary conditions for a productive and satisfied society. Social pressure led to governmental and regulatory limits on the prerogatives of business firms, to reduce the probability that extremely negative economic situations would occur again. Also, the growth in the power of organized labor required business firms to adjust their policies and practices relating to the ways in which employees were hired, compensated, promoted, and dismissed.

These shifts in the socioeconomic and political thinking were brought into colleges of business. At a minimum, business students were provided opportunities to discuss the pros and cons of some of the issues raised and to study the initiatives, policies, and programs suggested by the new social priorities. This involved debate over the proper role of the business institution in society and the appropriate degree of economic freedom business should have in dealing with its various clienteles, suppliers, and employees, and with minorities, other firms, and regulatory agencies. Therefore, the focus of business education on the objective analysis and study of resource acquisition, utilization, and distribution for profit began to include an analysis of how this resource flow process is affected by changing cultural and social values, priorities, and programs.

An array of views emerged through time, ranging from advocacy of the complete sanctity of the business institution to a call for more government regulation and even operation of business enterprises. Proponents on one extreme of the dialogue insisted that the proper role of business is business and the production of economic goods and services. Proponents on the other extreme were equally insistent that business is a social institution created by society, an institution that must produce economic goods and services in a socially responsible manner. The basic question is whether society can maintain the important benefits of the individual ethic and capitalism that productive individuals need and want, and yet satisfy the broader social values and priorities embodied in the social ethic and socialism, to provide minimal goods and services to the people less fortunate and less capable.

CULTURE, BUSINESS, AND MANAGEMENT IN TRANSITION

During the latter half of the twentieth century, a number of management philosophies have evolved in different cultural settings. As the business organization seeks to fulfill its economic mission, it must deal with the inherent diversity of peoples' values in the workplace. All of these philosophies are culturally based, which means the character of management practice stems from the value systems of society and, and in most cases, the emphasis on the individualistic versus the social ethic. Within this basic cultural setting, an organization applies and modifies technical, analytical, and managerial concepts and techniques as needed in its formal organization.

Bureaucratic Model

One important management philosophy is based on the bureaucratic model, which relies heavily on the use of formal authority. Its formal authority structures, policies, and rules are often accompanied by highly centralized planning and control systems. This type of management system does not provide many opportunities or incentives for individual innovation or input from lower organizational levels.

Various technical, analytical, and managerial concepts and techniques are usually designed at top management levels and implemented throughout the organization without substantial change. Thus the work level becomes removed from the decisionmaking level. Also, highly centralized planning and control systems may become cumbersome and ineffective in generating and implementing innovation, thus creating resistance to change.

On the other hand, some reasonable level of management bureaucracy is needed in all business organizations, to assign responsibility and delegate authority to use resources. It is necessary to effectively monitor, control, and adjust performance and goals. The other management philosophies, which are described below, do not discard bureaucracy in organizations, but shape it to include other social and behavioral factors.

European Industrial Democracy

European industrial democracy, or codetermination, is a second general type of management philosophy. It involves the workers in various aspects of management through specific legislation, usually in the collective bargaining process. Workers are represented on various management boards and work councils at all levels of the organization, including the board of directors of the firm. European industrial democracy provides for a very open type of organization, in which workers and managers formally and regularly meet to discuss (1) work design and performance, (2) managerial policies and practices, and (3) employee concerns and stockholder priorities. The various boards and councils provide a series of forums to integrate social and personal values and priorities with the economic goals of the firm and the employees.

Under the management philosophy of the European industrial democracy, greater emphasis is often placed on the social ethic than on the individual ethic, especially in periods of poor economic performance by the firm. In addition, in contrast with management systems relying more on the individualistic ethic, in an industrial democracy there tends to be a greater percentage of the firm's resources allocated to employee social welfare programs, such as health care, education, pay and leave benefits, and minimum wages.

European industrial democracy emerged as a major managerial philosophy in the aftermath of the second world war. The shared hardships gave more emphasis to the social ethic, which was carried forward into the workplace and influences political initiatives and business regulation at the local and national levels. In an industrial democracy, employees have a considerable voice in the work systems design and the resource distributions of their firms.

Management by Consensus

A third management philosophy is management by consensus, which stems from Japan's Ringi system and emphasizes familial relationships with the work organization. Similar to industrial democracy, it is a behavioral orientation that uses such concepts, such as participative management, quality circles, communications, and group dynamics. Management by consensus gained popularity because of its successful use in Japan, or conversely, Japan's success was attributed in part to the use of this management philosophy. In truth, management by consensus has also been used extensively in other countries, especially the United States. One key factor in its success in Japan has been the tradition of strong family loyalty in Japanese society, coupled with the perceived need for it in the economic and political chaos following the end of the second world war.

As used in Japan, management by consensus does not usually mean that all decisions are made by a formal employee vote. Instead, it provides information to the employees and gives them opportunities to endorse or provide input into the various decisions, design of work systems, and other political initiatives. As new generations of employees are drawn from the educational institutions in Japan, we can see some changes occurring in the employees'attitudes. For example, the younger employees are questioning the seniority system, which has been used extensively for promotion and compensation. They are now impatient for change and vocal about the need for it.

Worker Management

Worker management, a fourth management philosophy, is highly decentralized management. By law, it provides for the extensive involvement of workers in the management of the firm. It greatly expands the ideas of European industrial democracy and Japanese management by concensus by making workers responsible for "doing" and directly "managing" the means, conditions, and results of their labor. The worker management system often places a large burden on employees because of this dual role. This burden arises not only from the time involved but also from the special expertise required when dealing with issues and making decisions outside their respective disciplines.

The worker-management system tends to emphasize the social ethic, and the share of the firm's resources allocated to employee welfare tends to be large. Therefore, incentives for individual innovation and productivity are usually either less than needed or not be given a high priority. Also, worker-management systems tend to favor internal goals and quotas, reacting to environmental changes in a less than timely manner.

Hybrid Management

A fifth important system reflects a hybrid management philosophy. Management systems employed in the United States have typically been hybrid systems, a combination of organization and behavior concepts. There is much greater variation in the practices of managers of different firms and even within the same firm. Also, there has been experimentation with different managerial concepts, to improve organizational productivity and worker satisfaction. The cultural heritage of the United States has usually supported the individualistic ethic, while organizations have encouraged experimentation and change.

The hybrid model of management philosophy used in the United States is not a single model, but it does reflect numerous approaches to management through variations of bureaucracy, industrial democracy, management by consensus, and even worker-management. The choice of the approach or combination of approaches used is usually the individual manager's prerogative. However, in some organizations there are company-wide policies which require some common managerial practices involving employees in certain matters.

Culture and management in transition proceed as two highly interdependent thrusts through time. The practice of management is the synthesis of many disciplines and the product of cultural forces, as it attempts to provide the economic goods and services society demands. While the focus of management is in the economic realm, its actions are affected by social values and priorities. People are the primary means for management to fulfill its economic responsibility. The cultural fabric of society produces the values people bring into the workplace, which influence political regulatory systems affecting the economic environment.

In many cases, people's values change because of the failure of business to provide needed economic goods and services. For example, the changes during and after the major depression in the 1930s affected not only the balance of power of business, government, and organized labor, but they also moved employees away from the individualistic ethic toward the social ethic in the workplace. Needs for security and affiliation needs replaced the need to achieve and self-actualize. Government help became more popular than self-help, and the goals of profit and efficiency diminished somewhat in favor of social programs.

Today we can see distinct patterns of social values as they impact business and management. Even though the socialization process is important to many employees, the work ethic is still a dominant force in the workplace. Dominant among the forces that have emerged in recent years may be the entitlement idea, which people simply believe that society owes them a living. In many case these entitlement people have important skills, education and training, but they are not motivated; consequently, they present a major challenge for management. The entitlement people who are less capable pose a different kind of challenge for society and business, in that the greater opportunities provided for training or education may be able to move some of these people into the productive workforce.

Combinations of social values and economic initiatives are often translated into political institutions, initiatives, and government regulations. The political environment continues to be very crucial to business and management. Among other programs, foreign policy, trade policy, federal budget allocations, product regulations, employment practices, environmental protection measures, social welfare initiatives, and human rights and affirmative action procedures have emerged from the social sector through the political processes at the local, state, and national levels. Some of these become intertwined, to create major burdens for and increase the costs of business operations.

Because political initiatives and government

regulations continue to impact business and management, business firms and large industries continue to influence future political initiatives and regulations through two major concerns:

1. Extensive political and governmental control, regulation of business, and the implementation of costly social and environmental programs, once implemented, are difficult to remove, even though many people may agree they are no needed anymore.

2. These programs and initiatives may tend to dilate the individualistic ethic, diminishing the long-run competitive ability of business and management to provide the economic goods and services needed by society.

GENERAL GUIDELINES FOR CHANGE

Business enterprises operate in a changing socioeconomic and political environment to fulfill their economic mission for society. This means that they have gone beyond the point that they can expect to operate without continuous monitoring and regulation from the social and political sectors. Significant development of the business institution and management practices has occurred through the cultural rebirth, the industrial revolution, several major wars, and successive periods of recession and inflation. The more recent reforms occurring in Eastern Europe have emphasized the importance of the business institution to society, and the need to improve operations on society's behalf. The opening of Eastern Europe has prompted Western business firms to accelerate the development of new trade opportunities.

The changes underway in East European countries are similar to those that emerged during the cultural rebirth and the Industrial Revolution. For example, the Protestant ethic is being reemphasized as an important ingredient to increase individual efficiency, productivity, and innovation. As individual motivation and competition to achieve increase, the business enterprise is expected to become more efficient and productive. The market ethic is advocated as a vital mechanism to (1) enhance individual and enterprise effectiveness, (2) focus on the competitive position of the business enterprise, and (3) promote the country's economic performance on the international markets. Recognition of the liberty ethic is renewed through an emphasis on human rights. In addition, the need to permit individuals to enter into private contracts and to invest in and own property is recognized.

One valuable lesson from history reveals that from the range of choices available, even acknowledging the need for some level of social and political oversight and regulation, substantial support for the individualistic ethic must be provided. The method of distributing wealth must not be overshadowed by the need to develop new and better ways to produce it for society. If productive vitality and competitiveness are to be sustained, advertising must not be used as a substitute for research and development. Reliance on national planning systems is not a substitute for competition. Incentives and opportunities must continue to be made available to individuals and business enterprises, to promote the new ideas that emerge to sustain economic growth.

In countries in Eastern Europe, concurrent with these changes in business practices, is a considerable effort to design and deliver various types of business education programs in countries in Eastern Europe. These include MBA programs, management training courses for industry, and business courses at the bachelors' and high-school levels. There is a great urgency to design and deliver these business education programs, often employing faculty members from universities in the United States and other Western countries. Also, there seem to be high expectations that these business programs will increase business efficiency and productivity and improve individual motivation to work, innovate, and achieve. As a country implements these education programs, overall economic conditions are expected to improve. As with all programs involving change, the public is impatient for results, and if these results are not forthcoming in the short run, resistance to these new ideas can often be expected to surface.

The commitment to design and deliver business education programs to Eastern European countries must be accompanied by a commitment to the underlying tenets of the Protestant, market, and liberty ethics. In many countries in Eastern Europe, this commitment requires a substantial change in family and workplace values and perceptions of the types of socioeconomic and political institutions and initiatives needed. Moving from a society which has historically advocated the social ethic to one supportive of the

112

certainly requires an evolutionary, rather than an overnight, conversion process.

The introduction and use of market-system business and management education in East European countries will be influenced by (1) family and workplace values, (2) perceptions of the effectiveness of political institutions and processes, and (3) the different environment of each country. For example, countries moving from highly centralized national planning systems face a different set of problems from those practicing more decentralization in decisionmaking. The Soviet Union is an example of the former and Yugoslavia, of the latter.

From a macro perspective there are three important and interrelated movements in the socioeconomic and political system as a country changes it business education system and the way its business enterprises operate.

1. Support for the Protestant ethic as a mechanism to provide incentives for productivity and innovation;

2. Endorsement of the market ethic, to extend the individualistic ethic to the business enterprise level and to build a more competitive environment; and

3. Changes in political institutions and processes to include elements of the liberty ethic essential to the other two desired changes.

To be effective, the introduction of socioeconomic and political changes must include changes in these three areas, along with a general endorsement of them in the market-system business education programs. Changing a country's education system requires support and incentives from government budget agencies, industry groups, and university faculties. Rather than being committed to careers in government, business students must be committed to business as a career. They must remain in business education long enough to begin to influence business enterprise management.

In the interim, current industry managers must become exposed to these different business management concepts from several sources. For example, a series of regularly scheduled management training programs can be offered to specific industries, such as banking, manufacturing, and retailing. Selected managers can be given opportunities to visit Western firms in their respective industries, and they can be exposed to the different business practices of the Western firms that are either exporting to their firms or participating in joint ventures with them.

The process of change must follow several parallel avenues of management training courses, business degree programs, and visits from managers to other firms. These changes will eventually begin to reinforce each other, until they become more integrated into a recognizable and acceptable business discipline. As this discipline evolves, it should be tailored to the specific sociopolitical system involved. However, as business practice and education are modified to reflect the cultural fabric of the society, the basic foundation of Protestant, market, and liberty ethics should be maintained.

Adherence to these underlying tenets does not preclude adaptation of business programs, which is highly desirable, to respond to specific socioeconomic and political preferences and values. The differences in existing socioeconomic and political systems, processes, and structures are so significant as to require culturally literate business educators who are knowledgeable in market system business education concepts. Although faculty from other countries can help to design the curriculum and periodically teach short modules of the program, they should be used only in support roles. A primary objective is for the faculty in the host country to become self-sufficient in providing and managing the business education programs, using a variety of external support personnel as needed.

The purpose of business degree programs is (1) to educate people for future managerial and professional careers in business enterprises operating in a market-system environment and (2) to provide current managers and professionals with a series of short training courses relating to their industry, which focus on current business and management problems. These degree and training programs should focus on both corporate and small business enterprises, with an overall objective of improving the performance capacity of managers and professionals in regional, national, and international market-system environments. The proposed programs should also provide an awareness of important public policy issues and of the interdependencies of industry and government that may affect business and management.

While the current emphasis in Eastern Europe is on offering MBA degrees, it is highly desirable that business courses be offered at the undergraduate level so students can pursue concentrations or tracks in specialized areas of finance, marketing, accounting, information systems, and management. In many respects it may be more desirable to begin with the undergraduate curriculum before developing the master's degree in business.

Individuals currently working in industry should be provided opportunities to enroll in courses on specialized business topics, presented in segments of 3-10 days. Usually these individuals should be grouped by organizational level of management and by professional discipline within specific industries. Providing access to these new education programs for industry employees is essential for several reasons. Industry support is necessary to implement the needed socioeconomic and political changes. Business enterprises must be convinced of the importance of new business education concepts; otherwise these will be limited employment opportunities for business degree graduates. Also, with the aid of these informed employees, business enterprises will be better able to make the transition to the market-system environment.

A different type of organization may be needed in some countries (1) to develop and administer the business degree training programs in the major shift of emphasis to the market-system and (2) to encourage faculty to make career commitments to these programs. Initially, business degree and training programs may have to be organized and managed through a separate institute for business and management, by faculty from several disciplines in the various universities of the country. These faculty could have joint appointments to the new institute and to their current academic units in their respective universities.

The faculty of the Institute for Business and Management needs to develop a legacy of self-sufficient expertise, which would be enhanced by (1) sending students to the United States for doctoral study in business and (2) having current faculty in economics, organizational sciences, and political sciences adapt their expertise and perspectives to the market-system environment. Periodic participation by faculty from universities in other countries could first be used to seize the advantage of having special expertise and interests and to provide exposure to different socioeconomic and political perspectives. The comparative management dimension from this type of participation would be valuable.

The Institute for Business and Management needs to develop an advisory board of representatives from industry and government to serve as a forum to (1) resolve program issues; (2) assess accomplishments, needs, and opportunities; (3) communicate results; and (4) develop political support and funding for the degree and training programs. In the short run, these kinds of input from industry and government are essential.

There are several important advantages to establishing a new and separate institute, rather than an existing organization, to manage these business programs. This institute would reflect a major commitment to business and management programs, and this would facilitate interaction with industry, government, and other faculty and professionals in its funding proposals. In addition, a separate institute would provide more continuity of management in its programs and activities; this is needed for the long-term continuity of the changes being implemented. Eventually the institute would be merged into a separate college or academic unit, similar to other disciplines in a university.

Because of the magnitude of the task of introducing, developing, and delivering the business degree and training programs, a long-term commitment is required, along with substantial new resources. This task involves not only broad changes in social, economic, and political philosophy but requires the introduction of different kinds of educational concepts, techniques, and delivery systems.

SUMMARY

Since the beginning of the Industrial Revolution, the dominant theme of business education and practice in the Western world has been centered on the three tenets emerging from the cultural rebirth: the Protestant, market, and liberty ethics. Industry and business schools became partners in the development and testing of business and management theory and concepts. Business schools became major instruments of socioeconomic and political reform, and in some cases this role was a reactive one, because education programs adapted to changes in the environment. Business schools sometimes played a pro-active role in the development and promotion of new theories, concepts, and ideas.

The developments in Eastern Europe provide an

important challenge for university education programs in these countries, as their resources must be effectively applied to the needs of changing socioeconomic and political systems and initiatives. This transition involves a shift toward the tenets of the Protestant, market, and liberty ethics. In many cases it deals with changing individual and family workplace values, as well as socioeconomic and political institutions and processes. The task involves the reeducation of society at all levels and will require a long transition period.

The primary responsibility for changing and delivering new education programs should lie with the faculty from within the country involved. This is highly desirable, because the faculty must be culturally literate. Although faculty from other countries may be used in temporary support roles, the country must build self-sufficiency in faculty, libraries, and budgets.

The initial recipients of the new business education programs must include two groups: (1) current key employees in industry must access business training programs, and (2) university students must be encouraged to pursue careers in business. To facilitate inclusion of these groups, business courses and degree programs must be made available to both undergraduate and graduate students.

The effectiveness of the business education programs will not be measureable immediately, and some segments may undergo modifications in the future. Changes in the socioeconomic and political institutions and processes, along with changes in business practice, will shape these programs over time; the experimentation occurring should not seriously dilute the Protestant, market, and liberty ethics.

9

The System of Self-Management
Anton Vratusa

The purpose of this chapter is to present some views on the development of the Yugoslav system of self-management, to identify the major causes of its later erosion, and to indicate possible options for positive future development. The intention is to engage the academic community in an unbiased discussion about the "Yugoslav way to socialism" while the citizens and member-nations of the Yugoslav plurinational federation are confronted with the imminent need to construct a new historic agreement as a foundation for their common future.

A question might be raised about the logic of such an effort when practically all the aspects of the Yugoslav social order that were based on socialist self-management have become objects of doubt, reevaluation, or general rejection. Under the present circumstances, such an undertaking is difficult and risky, but on the other hand, the existing confusion and uncertainty require that a scientific effort be made to identify the essence of the crises, which may yield some direction on how to overcome the current deadlock.

When confronted with various alternatives, it is important to determine what will have a beneficial effect on future socioeconomic, political, and cultural development. It is equally relevant to know whether the occurring phenomena are temporary upheavals in the contemporary crises or whether they reflect long-term conflicts in Yugoslavia and the world community.

The origins of the Yugoslav system of self-management can be traced to the legendary 1941-45 struggle against foreign invaders for self-defense and liberation of the Yugoslav people and nations.

The genuine organs of self-management during the National Liberation War were the workers' councils in factories and the national liberation committees operating on liberated and occupied territory. These groups were revolutionary instruments enabling workers and the people to make direct and free decisions on everyday issues and on the needs of the National Liberation Army units. When invaders fragmented the Yugoslav territory, the common idea of a joined armed resistance to the invaders and the building of a new Yugoslavia stimulated a variety of independently supported self-reliant struggles adapted to local situations. The self-management-based organizations functioned not only to inspire and unify people but to induce them to participate actively in social affairs.

During the first years after the liberation of the country, self-management practice was limited to (1) various types of workers and trade union representatives as consultants to enterprises and institutions and (2) certain forms of people's self-management in neighborhood communities and municipalities. This limitation of self-management practice resulted from the concentration and centralized administration of available resources which was intended to speed up the industrialization of the country; from the low level of economic development; from state ownership; and from the influence of the Soviet sociopolitical system.

The unanimous resistence to the concentric military, political, and economic pressure exercised upon Yugoslavia by Stalin and his East-European Cominform followers (1948-53) produced favorable conditions for a full implementation of the self-management concept and its gradual transformation into a global system of autonomous decisionmaking by workers about their work and workplaces. As a matter of fact, self-management democracy was a major source of encouragement to the Yugoslav people during those years. By defending their country's independence, they were defending their own individual and collective right to decide autonomously about the results of their work and to distribute national resources.

The cornerstone of the self-managed production relations system was laid down in 1950 with the adoption by the Federal Assembly of the Law on Transfer of the Right of Management to Workers in State-Owned Enterprises and in their Higher Economic Association. Two years later, at its Sixth Congress, the Communist Party of Yugoslavia--the leading political force and the organizer of the National Liberation Movement and of the socialist reconstruction of the country--decided to transform itself into the League of Communists. It did this to formally demonstrate its determination to fulfill its role through ideological and political leadership, based on the strength of arguments, not on its position as the party in power. With this intent, the decision to separate the party from the state was proclaimed. An accumulation of executive power by leading personalities, except Tito, was prohibited, and political service was limited to two consecutive terms. Similar democratization decisions in the legal and political system were sanctioned the next year by the Constitutional Law of 1953.

In the same spirit, councils as advisory bodies to the local government were established on the commune (municipality) and district levels to ensure democratic participation by neighborhood communities in the decisions on common interest issues. The introduction of producers as the second chamber in the structure of the commune and district people's committee was intended to enable workers to exercise direct influence from their own workplaces through their elected factory representatives as members of the mentioned organs. As a matter of fact, establishing the chamber of producers was the first decisive step in the process to building an integrated system of self-management in the political system of Yugoslavia. However, the main macroeconomic decisions remained with the central state and party organs.

At the Seventh Congress of the League of Communists in 1958, the new program was adopted. It promoted self-management and socialist democracy through direct participation in decisionmaking or through election of delegates to workers' councils, neighborhood communities, and municipality assemblies. These representative bodies represented a legal basis for electing delegates to the assemblies of republics and autonomous regions. The constitution of 1963 brought the system of self-management to completion in the whole social order, from the socially owned enterprises and neighborhood communities to the federal assembly.

Taking the system of self-management in Yugoslavia as the sociopolitical source of human rights and liberties, the League of Communists had the foresight to develop a no-party political system as a humane and democratic alternative to both systems (the one-party and the pluriparty). Consequently, Yugoslavia, as a member of the non-aligned movement, was able to serve as an independent international force in a world divided by self-interest groups and military and political blocs.

The basic socioeconomic and political goal of self-management was to put any worker or citizen, individually or as a member of a working or people's community, in a position to make decisions and choices based on his or her own interests and responsibility to fellow workers, citizens, and the community at large, regardless of party affiliation. The problem with an indispensable democratic control over those in political power was that it had to be matched with the creation of a climate responsive to the free development of a socialist alliance of working people. This had to be an all-embracing democratic front for citizens regardless of their philosophical, religious, or political convictions or racial/national origin. The Union of Socialist Youth was conceived as a general autonomous association of youth, to perform a similar function as an instrument of influence and control in the hands of the younger generation. Under these circumstances the confederation of trade unions of Yugoslavia, an arm of the working class, was supposed to exercise democratic control and to develop worker consciousness and culture. It was to protect the workers' interests against bureaucratic arbitrariness and the common interests of the whole community against individual or collective selfishness and social parasitism.

In 1963 the second constitution of Yugoslavia introduced the Chambers of Associated Labor throughout the system, from the commune (lowest level) to the federal assembly (highest level). The dynamic growth of the national economy after the introduction of self-management suggested its further progress. However, problems with the national economy were generated by a central planning system focused on the growing concern over (1) the role of the market, (2) the requirements of economic law, and (3) the development of a unified system of self-management from above without consideration of the different levels of economic development in various regions of the country. A decline in work productivity began, accompanied by obvious signs of dissatisfaction among workers. Underestimation of the plurinational structure of the Yugoslav community and an increasing disregard for the pluralism of the interests of the nations and nationalities in Yugoslavia fueled mounting intranational tensions and conflicts.

The first comprehensive social and economic reform was launched in 1965, although it never accomplished its major goals. It was intended to (1) put the Yugoslav economy on a healthy and efficient economic basis through optimal use of material and financial resources, regardless of ownerships relations; (2) motivate labor and entrepreneurial management and free competition on the national and international markets; and (3) democratically integrate the national economy on a unified Yugoslav market on self-management principles, with mutual solidarity and respect for the plurinational interests of the Yugoslav community of equal nations.

The monopolistic position of the socially owned sector of the national economy continued to keep large resources in other ownership forms either idle or underemployed. These problems also caused economic inefficiency and stagnations in the socially owned sector itself.

The system continued to function without economic coercion for all who were entrusted to use socially owned resources, who were expected to guarantee optimal economic, financial, and social development results through creative management and motivated labor. In other words, the primary cause of the inefficiency of the Yugoslav model of self-management, residing within the system itself, remained untouched. Consequently, socially owned undertakings were unable to generate a higher level of productivity in work or to compete efficiently on the market with enterprises in private or cooperative ownership or on the international market. Under these circumstances, the Yugoslav national economy was not able to maintain normal production and indispensable capital accumulation, nor to satisfy the rapidly increasing social needs, which were the basis of liberal social legislation requiring expenditure for a social standard beyond the capability of the existing level of labor productivity.

The state additionally increased its direct intervention in enterprise management through (1) a new centralization of the national economy, (2) very detailed legislative provisions, and (3) administrative interference into everyday management issues. There was growing concern about the preservation of social peace in the country and about keeping social and political developments under control, using the prevailing administrative and repressive measures.

Student demonstrations in 1968 made the state and political authorities even more suspicious and restrictive. In retrospect, it seems that these events involving student action were the last warning to the League of Communists to go back to its own decisions at the Sixth Congress in 1952 and to implement them consistently in the spirit of the late 1940s and the early 1950s, during the struggle against Stalin's hegemony.

If the democratic basis of the whole political system had been broadened, the League of Communists might have been able to inspire new strength and motivation for self-management and to regain the confidence of the people. However, the ever worsening economic and social climate of the country, plus the outbreak of intranational conflicts on the crest of a new nationalistic euphoria, caused the league to decide differently. It renewed and strengthened its links with state power, underestimating the growing demand for democratization of the country.

These developments spawned greater state and political bureaucratic monopolistic power. They progressively suffocated labor's incentive and motivation and undermined the individual and collective sense of responsibility. The decentralized and polycentric process of decisionmaking was greatly reduced, making the system more vulnerable to corruption. The competence of the workers' councils and other organs of self-management was gradually eroding. Workers were rapidly loosing interest in these activities. Differences and disputes between management and the work force were growing, in the form of frequent strikes and public demonstrations. The hired-labor mentality was a dark cloud on the horizon and extinguished hopes that had been initiated and encouraged by the idea and practice of self-management.

Increasing intervention by the state in the national economy, strengthening the authority of the federation over the expenses of the constituent republics and overemphasizing a particular national/republic economy, aggravated the deep nationalistic clashes in the plurinational community of Yugoslavia. Protectionist and discriminatory measures were increasingly undertaken against each other by the individual republics. This disrupted the integrity of the unified market of the country. Opposition to the principle of consensus, even when the vital interests of the individual nation/republic were in question, served to strengthen centrifugal tendencies, undermining mutual confidence among the nations and republics. The dilemma about federation, as opposed to confederation, which is separation on the basis of the right self-determination of nations, represents one of the deepest divisions in the history of Yugoslavia. This stimulates the desire to reinforce the federation by an administrative centralization of the system under the hegemony of the most numerous nation, on the one hand, and more strident demands for full sovereignty and independence for the majority of smaller nations, on the other.

Difficulties arose on the political level with the monopolistic position of the League of Communists, which left practically no room for alternative options, either within the league or in the community. The league gradually became a state party with a full political monopoly.

In this political climate, the function of the Socialist Alliance of the Working People was, in practice, to transmit the will of the league. Relations in the neighborhood communities were the exception, because the organizations of the Socialist Alliance continued to initiate many activities that addressed human needs. The alliance assumed the role of a democratic political and cultural educator, teaching self-management, solidarity, and self-reliance. The trade unions played a more objective and independent role, for within the framework of the self-management system they might have accomplished a great deal. However, bureaucracy prevailed, causing many trade union organs or organizations and many trade union leaders to prefer a "backseat" role in the shadow of the League of Communists and enterprise management, rather than risk making active attempts to resolve the people's social and related problems.

The conceptual interaction between the League of Communists and state power was also reflected in the Third Constitution of Yugoslavia (1974). The League and other sociopolitical organizations were incorporated in the preambula of the constitution as established forces of socialism. When there was broad decentralization into the community, the intent was to ensure a corresponding position for the League of Communists, to enable it to act as a cohesive force safeguarding the control of the cental party and state organs over relations and processes in the whole country. However, in actuality the political monopoly of the league and its embodiment in the constitution only served to strengthen its autocratic power over the whole social system. In the absence of effective democratic control and institutionalized opposition within the framework of the existing social system, such a constitutional position by the League of Communists led to the self-distruction of the league itself, throwing a sinister shadow across the self-management system.

Edvard Kardelj, the architect of the system of self-management democracy in Yugoslavia, was aware of the danger. For years he strived to generate a democratic and humane approach through the development of the system of self-management and to prevent the growth of bureaucracy in the country. On several occasions he was warned that self-management in Yugoslavia was still at the starting line. He was told that it could progress only in a democratic and political environment. Self-management requires a climate of mutual responsibility based on consciousness and solidarity, warned someone, while another considered a step-by-step process indispensable to the maintenance of contact with the economic, social, and cultural reality. Although physically exhaused by a long serious illness (cancer), he wrote the study "Development of the Political System of Socialist Self-Management" in 1977. This was his philosophical credo, which echoed through the world. In it he detailed the complex dangers facing the self-management system in Yugoslavia.

In an analysis of democracy in a socialist society, Kardelj explained the democratic socialism of self-management interests as a new form of the democratic political system. He formulated some far-reaching recommendations and practical guidelines for a policy to further improve the political system of self-management democracy in Yugoslavia. He recognized the democratic achievements of mankind within the system of pluriparty parliamentary democracy. However, in view of the wide, revolutionary social and political changes in Yugoslavia during the National Liberation War, and in view of the postwar development and the strategic orientation of the self-management socialist democracy, he remained convinced that the actual introduction of a pluriparty political system would mean a step backwards. Had he been fortunate enough to continue his visionary architecture, subsequent events would have served as reminders of his fervent hopes and thoughts at the beginning of the democratic transformation of the League of Communists in the early 1950s.

Several weeks before he died in February 1979,

Kardelj was unhappy to learn that a one-year mandate principle had been introduced for the function of the chairman in organs of the political and state collective leadership (the exception being Tito, who was almost 90 years old) and in other areas, without the possibility of reelection. This was issued under the pretext of ensuring a further democratization of the political system and to prevent the misuse of power, but it was an unfortunate step. In the actual Yugoslav environment, it led to a further erosion of the system and paved the way to personal and group rivalries among the political and state bureaucracies of the constituent republics and autonomous regions levels. Negative reactions to the system's performance were registered at all levels, especially in the political vacuum after Tito's death in May 1980. Abuse of power cannot be prevented by the mandate limitation alone. There must be genuine transparency of the government and the whole political system, free circulation of information, competent and motivated participation by the people in decisionmaking efficient democratic control over the activity of all of public functionaries, and direct accountability of the government to the electorates.

Increasing internal difficulties and conflicts had a negative impact on Yugoslavia's activities on an international level. Its capacity to participate actively in international relations and to adapt to changes in the world diminished, and autarchic tendencies surfaced with strength and vigor. Errors in economic and social policy were mounting to destroy self-management and the achievements of the working people.

Because of this erosion in the institutions of self-management democracy, the recovery and reaffirmation of progressive development in Yugoslavia may be slow and painful. There is deep disappointment and demoralization in the ranks of the League of Communists, and the whole population is dissatisfied with the general economic, social, and political crisis in the country and the vengeful attitudes of some in the newly involved circles of power. The collapse of the socialist systems in Central and East-European countries, which has been interpreted in many circles as the end of socialism, may cause discontent and disorientation. However, thanks to achievements based on a self-managed socialist democracy, the unique events in Yugoslavia may offer a more favorable avenue for recovery and progress.

Pertinent questions circulating in Yugoslavia and abroad relate to the sociohistorical vehicles that caused the Yugoslav system of self-management to go awry. What are the authentic origins of the current political, economic, and moral crisis? Was the crisis brought about because, for the first time in history, the idea of self-management was implemented in theory and practice, to serve as the socioeconomic base of a socialist democracy?

No doubt, the historic undertaking to build a political system of socialist self-management, which required a high level of labor culture, consciousness, self-discipline, and responsibility, and to build it in an economically underdeveloped country, without a democratic political tradition, in a pluri-national federation, and generally unfriendly international environment, was a bold and risky undertaking.

The average per capita national income in Yugoslavia after the liberation was about $350 U.S. The difference between the least developed region (Kosovo) and the most developed region (Slovenia) was 1:7. The peasant population represented about 75 percent of the total population, but today, it is not more than 25 percent. The percentage of illiterate people was high, about 70 percent, in Kosovo, but only 3 percent in Slovenia. Agriculture represented about 65 percent of the total national income, and less than 25 percent. More than two-thirds of the workers in industry were the first-generation workers, while the majority were farming on the side, on land they owned.

In this sociohistoric climate there was only a small number of workers who could actively and competently participate in the self-management decisionmaking process. In addition, the continued high concentration of resources and administrative redistribution by the state reduced the competence of the workers' councils to such a degree that their decisions almost never went beyond the setting of simple production limits. Decisions about expanded production remained completely in the hands of the political and administrative authorities. Nevertheless, there was a permanent and impressive number of success stories about self-managed socially-owned prevailingly medium-sized enterprises. It is true, however, that the majority of these enterprises belonged to the economically more developed regions of Yugoslavia, which had a rather homogeneous labor structure and a relatively higher level of skills, know-how, and work ethic.

The monopoly on social ownership relations represented the major limiting factor, not only to the efficacy, but to the efficiency of the self-management system and the whole national economy. Moreover, the essence of social ownership had never been clearly or legally defined. This ambiguity was a permanent source of waste of socially-owned resources and the national income. Socially-owned enterprises were usually never compelled to compete for their income on the market, because their economic difficulties were resolved when they occurred, usually through party and state interventions.

On the one hand, there was a continuous process of privatization of the results of common efforts and socialization of losses from individual or collective performance. The expenses of successful undertakings were not regarded as anyone's responsibility. On the other hand, the monopoly on the social ownership relations total, although about 80 percent of arable land, crafts, small shops, and services remained in private ownership. The monopolistic position of socially-owned enterprises, and a protectionist policy in favor of enterprises in social ownership alone, narrowed the chances of undertakings based on resources in private and cooperative ownership. Further, the nonexistence of a free market of capital, goods, and labor worked against individual and collective motivation, incentive, and creativity. At the same time, it strengthened social parasitism.

In 1989 the proclamation introducing ownership pluralism was generally welcomed. It stimulated a wave of legislative measures intended to destroy the material and political basis for the self-management system. These measures met with serious resistance among workers or in the community.

Another factor limiting the success of the management system was the vulnerability of the concept itself and the failure of practical implementation. The structure of the organs of self-were prescribed by law or government decrees and state administrative rules. This left practically no room for creative action by the self-management organs. Such a dense forest of regulations made competent decisionmaking by workers' councils very questionable, opening up a Pandora's Box of speculations, manipulations, and misuse. This produced gray areas of the collective responsibility within the various organs and society.

Still another important limiting factor was the lack of a genuine political democracy. The concept of self-management is by its very nature protective of rights and freedoms. Its human and liberating essence can only reach fruition if the working man is able to exert influence from the work place and neighborhood by participating in social affairs directly, or indirectly through his delegates in the assemblies on all community levels. However, because of the degree of bureaucracy of the League of Communists and decentralized state bureaucratism on the constituent republic and municipal levels, the necessary channels for a free flow of the information needed for exercising self-management rights were closed. This confined and limited self-management to the enterprises and institutions.

Under the burden of its own degeneration, and with mounting pressure from a dogmatic and bureaucratic environment, self-management lost its own original socioeconomic and political liberation power. Actually, when faced with accumulated conflicts and decay in everyday life and practice, the self-management system needed the permanent support of the existing party and state power. It became and more evident that if the concept of a democratic pluralism of self-managed interests were to retain its sense of direction, it would have to interact with the prevailing democratic political pluralism and with ideological preconceptions about the democratic and cultural essence of the system of parliamentary pluriparty democracy.

The result was a breakthrough, from three major factors: (1) the wave of democratization in a number of Central and East European countries, a general easing of world tensions, especially in Europe, and the revolt of the people of Yugoslavia against the political monopoly of the League of Communists. The league's marriage to the state and its policies had led the country into economic stagnation, extensive foreign debt, and international isolation. As the result of general, free, and secret elections, a parliamentary pluriparty political system was introduced in Slovenia and Croatia in spring 1990. By late 1990, this system was expected to become a reality throughout Yugoslavia, in a pattern of democratization.

However, all of these reforms will not eliminate the causes of the crisis unless a new democratic agreement can be reached among the sovereign nations of Yugoslavia. Parallel to this would be consistent, democratic reform throughout the whole social structure, from the bottom to the top. Basic human rights and liberties would have to be guaranteed for every individual and group, and sovereignty and equality would have to be guaranteed for all nations. There must be a new historic agreement among the nations of Yugoslavia, based on human rights, parliamentary democratic ownership pluralism, market economy national sovereignty, good neighbor policies, open frontiers, and respect for the historic democratic achievements of the National Liberation War and positive postwar development. Only such an agreement will inspire the people and nations of Yugoslavia to combine their efforts and mobilize their talents, in order to set the stage for living together in the future.

The League of Communists and the government of Yugoslavia won the battle with Stalin for autonomy; however, the Yugoslav leadership has not won the war against Stalinism. Traces of orthodoxy persist in the minds of most leaders, trained in the spirit of obedience to the authority of the Communist International and loyalty to the first socialist state in the world, under permanent pressure by imperalist powers after WWI. At that time, all democratically oriented elements in the kingdom of Yugoslavia were severely persecuted. This was permanently limiting in the development of the present leaders, both psychologically and morally, as seen in their perceptions of the development of the self-management system itself and the democratization process in general. The policy of complete isolation that was practiced by all communists' and workers' parties loyal to Moscow during the five-year plus dispute with Stalin and his followers, and the accusations of being called revisionists, had a similar impact on the perceptions of many Yugoslav leaders. A divorce from the Stalinist mentality never took place, and this has been the major barrier to the development of a genuine socialist democracy, although it is true that self-management as a system and practice has left a deep imprint on people's minds.

The need for radical changes in the constitution, legal, and political systems should not be a pretext for the negations of all past achievements, or for an uncritical imitation of foreign models. Foreign practices should not be mechanically transplanted models. Foreign practices should not be mechanically transplanted into Yugoslav society without taking the existing sociohistorical and cultural differences into account. A comprehensive and objective analysis of events and relations should be made, to ascertain which elements in the existing social, cultural, and political system can maintain the positive achievements of past development and sustain future democratic growth.

The current relationship of forces in Yugoslavia and the actual level of development require a new approach. What is most important is not to lose sight of the democratic and humanist essence of self-management in the struggle for human rights and freedom. At the same time, it is vital to free self-management and the participatory practice of their dogmatic burdens and economic inefficiency, and to adapt their content, structure, and organizational forms to correspond with the emerging system of ownership pluralism and the general economic, political, cultural, and moral mentality. Under these conditions, it is possible to develop self-management participation in Yugoslavia as an instrument for direct and active influence by workers and citizens on social affairs and to overcome the narrow new trends in future development regulation.

In the Yugoslav experience, the concept of a uniform and integrated system of self-management was confronted by insurmountable obstacles even in an integrated social ownership system. It would not be wise to legally obligate all self-managed, socially owned enterprises to become enterprises with mixed ownership. The proclaimed equality of all ownership forms--public, private, cooperative, mixed, and social--would be implemented. If a socially owned enterprise is producing with optimal results, including a steady increase in accumulation, and if the workers are interested and able to continue effectively, why should they be compelled to replace self-management with management forms similar to state or private ownership relations?

These two facts should be kept in mind:

1. The principles of self-management and other forms of participation in decisionmaking are recognized in various contemporary social systems as democratic and civilized.

2. People in the contemporary world have become aware of certain human freedoms and rights-- without individual socioeconomic security-- that are by their very nature abstract.

In the final analysis, the content and vitality of self-management and the different forms of active participation in Yugoslavia will depend on more free development of democracy and culture in the whole

132

community. Within this context, the following criteria are especially important as a framework for democracy and civilized behavior:

- A socioeconomic system based on ownership pluralism and equal legal safeguards for all forms of ownership rights, free entrepreneurship, and competition in a free market; a management system based on motivated self-management or participatory decisionmaking. The role of the state in the national economy should be limited in order to safeguard mutual rights and obligations in production and labor relations. The state should promote an environment of economic and financial stability, with optimal use of natural resources and free access to the international market and the achievements of modern science, technology, and civilization.

- The guarantee of human freedom and rights and the promotion of socioeconomic, political, and cultural conditions conducive to the implementation of these rights and freedoms on a democratic level. This would include the freedom to pursue activities promoting self-management participation and self-government in all areas of social activity.

- A democratic political system based on direct, free, and secret elections and a social order with legally shared responsibilities.

- A national economy and community that are open to contemporary world currents and developments of a scientific, technological, economic, and cultural nature. This would include active involvement in the European and global democratic processes for world peace and security.

10

Foreign Capital, Private Property, and the Firm

Stojan Bulat

The goal of many of Yugoslavia's post-World War II political and economic reforms has been to improve the function of the economic system and to increase democracy in political life. In altering an economic and political system based on the Soviet model, Yugoslavia has been in sharp contrast with other socialist countries, which have had to follow the Soviet principles of state-owned means of production; central planning; an almost nonexistent market; primacy of social interests over the interests of the individual; and monopoly of one party, the Communist Party.

While the reforms in Yugoslavia were somewhat successful, they could not improve the functioning of the overall system, which was seemingly beyond repair. The inefficiency of these reforms came from ideological prejudice and mistaken premises, which obstructed the attempted reforms in every area. These ideological obstructions involved such basic tenets as social ownership of the means of production necessary for continuing to give the Communist Party the leading role in all economic and political decisionmaking, especially planning and the selection of priorities in development policy.

The positive results of these reforms were visible in the increasing role of the market mechanism in allocating resources. Despite these improvements, it was not until the most recent reforms that significant progress was made toward adopting a market mechanism for all production factors, a mechanism based on the requirements of a modern market, on the micro- and macroeconomic elements of economic policy along market principles. The present reforms in Yugoslavia, as in other socialist countries, are significantly different from prior attempts at reform, as experience indicates the need to reform the entire system rather than repair it or make small cosmetic changes to it.

This means that socialism can no longer be identified solely with social property and state-owned means of production. This is an attack on the main ideological and political premises that would interfere with pluralism of ownership. By pluralism of ownership, I mean equal status for all types of ownership in the socioeconomic system. Pluralism of ownership also requires political pluralism as an institutional framework of political democracy, to ensure and maintain basic human rights and freedom.

Critics of socialism were right in saying that the concept of a socialist economy is irrational and inefficient in the long run. Among these critics, two of the most prominent were the social theorists Ludvig von Mizes and Fredrich A. von Hayek. In the 1920s, when the Soviet Union's socialist economy was in its infancy, these theorists had the foresight to visualize many of the irrationalities and the undesirable results such a system would produce; they were especially mindful of the danger of creating a proliferating bureaucratic system.

Frequent reforms are proof of the inefficiency and dysfunction of the institutional framework that socialist economies operate in and the serious defects of their basic implementation concepts.

We are now convinced that the small changes being made in many socialist societies could have resulted neither in the transformation of the system nor in the eradication of the cumulative problems inherent in such a system. There is momentum for the opinion that the changes have to be deep and significant to effect substantial improvements in the basic elements of the system. But there are barriers in the way of those efforts because in the countries now undertaking such drastic changes there is general lack of knowledge to carry out the reforms and fear of social unrest.

Not only is egalitarianism one of the basic tenets of socialism, but it imposes one of the greatest barriers to the speed and magnitude of reforms in socialist countries. It is dangerous to an economy's efficiency and creativity, for in the long run it stifles initiative, decreasing the entire productivity of labor. On the other hand, market forces and pluralism of ownership lead to an increase in productivity.

Currently, substantial reform in all socialist

countries, including Yugoslavia, points toward a market economy. However, there are still different concepts of reform and especially of the role of the market mechanism. Specifically, when the question of a market economy and market mechanism is analyzed, differences in opinion arise about the role and character of a modern market. There are those who strongly advocate only market forces but either do not give a precise definition of the type of market they have in mind or describe a type of market that is not consistent with the modern market structure. The market forces do not operate in the same way as those in the nineteenth-century model.

Even in Western market countries, there is still debate among the different economic schools about the best market models to use for analyzing real economic life. Because of this, each of these countries has its own concept of the institutional framework, methods, and degrees of government regulation needed in the economic system. There is real controversy over (1) the types of instruments best suited for macroeconomic policy, (2) the performance of those instruments in certain development periods, (3) the best methods of intervention, and (4) the system and degree of regulation or deregulation of the economic sector that is most favorable to economic and social development.

Government intervention in the economic affairs of Yugoslavia faces significant problems inherent in the existing political system. Although Yugoslavia was the first socialist country to undertake reform and decentralization of economic decisionmaking and to abolish the role of central planning, she did not give enterprises independence in their market behavior. Instead of imposing federal administrative intervention, which was known to be inefficient, more administrative intervention was introduced on the level of the republics, provinces, and even communes and local authorities. Now there is much more, rather than less, government intervention at the different levels. This level of intervention, especially at the local level, exists in no other market economy.

Therefore, as a precondition, reforms to the political system, along with free and multiparty elections, should accelerate implementation of economic reforms. It is primarily necessary to write about and adopt a new constitution that will make Yugoslavia a modern federation. The 1974 constitution is not only a confused mixture of confederal and federal solutions but a source of many problems in political decisionmaking that are unknown in any other contemporary federal state. In addition, in the constitution of 1974, there is unnecessary regulation of economic life based on consensus, a practice that blocks normal decisionmaking in both economic matters and political affairs.

As a part of great economic and constitutional crisis in Yugoslavia, there is debate over the necessity for a new constitution and a new political system. There are still coalitions contending that Yugoslavia should be a federation, with a precisely defined role for the federal government and its performance in the federal units. Some favor a confederal framework, with relations among the members of the present federation. While we are witnessing a process of integration and creation of more concrete relations among the countries of the European Community and the expectation of a united federation of European countries with a single market, we also see disintegration and the formation of separate states and mini-states in Yugoslavia, and also in the Soviet Union.

Confederation is practically nonexistent as a link between different states in the modern world. Even Switzerland is a confederation in name only, and all other solutions are federal. The history of confederal countries and their social development belongs to the Middle Ages. Most of the confederations of the past either became federations or ceased to be linked.

At times Yugoslavia, as a federation, is confronted with major problems because of inter-republic, national, religious, and ethnic conflicts of such magnitude as to threaten civil war. Such a conflict could then spread to other parts of Europe, leading to confrontation on an international scale. One might ask, Who takes responsibility for the creation of this crisis? The answer would be those who gained power and privileges in the federal units, such as the republics and autonomous provinces, and then, at the expense of the common interests of the people of Yugoslavia, incited nationalistic and chauvinistic passions among the peoples of those regions.

Certainly the long-term economic and political interests of Yugoslavia would be on the side of saving a united Yugoslavia, with its present borders, as a federal country. Of course, the new constitution should secure to the federal government and its authority a certain minimum of necessary federal tools to regulate the macroeconomic policy.

138

Since their formation, most of the federated
countries that make up Yugoslavia have experienced
disputes between federal power and the power of the
federal units. (I cannot discuss all of these
aspects in detail in this chapter.) The minimum
federal power necessary for the normal function of a
market economy should be the authority to create
fiscal, monetary, and foreign trade regulations to
permit the function of a single market.
Consequently, the success of economic reform will
depend on the democratic reform of the political
system, which should facilitate fundamental changes
to the economic system.

In the Yugoslav constitution of 1974, there were
many regulations detailing the way the economic
system should operate and the way economic
regulations were really counterproductive, since
changes in the economic system always necessitated
changes in the constitution. Changes to the
constitution were not always easy--a state of affairs
causing frequent constitutional crises. I believe
that economic regulations and intervention should be
implemented by legislative procedure.

Over the past two decades there have been shocks to
the Yugoslav economy and society from the expanding
social crises. Therefore, the new phase of reform
cannot be merely a face-lift but rather must be a
reexamination of the fundamentals of the system. It
can take time to make drastic changes; the concept of
social ownership may have to be left as the
irreplaceable assumption. Now we have the treatment
of social property as social capital, not just as
free goods. Furthermore, the way is open to a market
evaluation of all production factors, reaffirmation
of property pluralism, and the creation of new
conditions for competition between different types of
ownership. In other words, we are witnessing the
revocation of many of the limitations on private
ownership in scope of production, number of
employees, ownership of buildings and equipment, and
also foreign investment. Foreign citizens are now
allowed to form enterprises and invest their capital,
with none of the limitations imposed until now on the
percentage of ownership of enterprises.
Realistically, they may found their own enterprises,
or buy existing enterprises.

That is the reason that the complex structure of
ownership is at the center of the debate about
reform. The search is on for the best ways to
transform property, especially private property,
which of course means increasing the role of the

139

market.

Social ownership was integrated as state ownership; although a later attempt was made to transform it back into social ownership, the attempt really did not succeed economically. State domination of social ownership was a serious obstacle to the development of a proper market economy. Theoretically, social ownership never was developed as a positive concept to function without problems; it was really a concept of "nonownership."

The main questions confronting social ownership were how to motivate and instill economic responsibility for the efficient use of resources through means-of-production and economy-of-labor costs. If competition among between different types of ownership can be successfully established in Yugoslavia, then a flexible mechanism can be developed to facilitate the transformation between types of ownership; this should help cure socialism's ills.

A process by which unsuccessful enterprises can be taken over by the successful is now possible because of new reforms. Empirical evidence should lead to wider transactions of capital between different types of ownership. The main precondition for such a process is the development of a financial market and stock exchange as the main instruments to mobilize capital flow, which would then yield a higher return. Unfortunately, the stock and financial markets and the market for corporate securities are now in the elementary stages.

The present economic reforms should develop an adequate concept of social ownership transformation by identifying the title of that ownership. This can be partially accomplished by selling social enterprises as if they were state-owned. The money that comes from these transactions then goes into funds for development of the republics and provinces.

It has been suggested that social enterprises should issue shares to employed people as one of the variants; the other is that the shares should be issued to the entire population. In essence, the second variant is based on the concept that social ownership belongs to the entire population, pointing out that this is more justified. Both of these variants, however, would be difficult to implement.

The federal government places great importance on transformation of ownership, for the entire concept of reform is based on it. As a result, the rights of managers in decisionmaking processes have broadened significantly, with the distinction made between "managing and self-managing." In that respect there are still some limitations, imposed by the concept of self-management, that bear further examination.

The federal government faces resistance to these changes, because to increase efficiency in the entire performance of the economy, it must go directly to reprivatization of many sectors of the economy, which draws strong opposition from certain groups. Therefore, if the interest from foreign capital is not enough to buy domestic enterprises, then private domestic sources must oversee the transformation. This situation can lead to a possible depreciation in the prices of the enterprises to be sold. It also may lead to criminal activities at the management level or on the part of the new owners of these enterprises. This type of criminal activity has already occurred in Hungary and Poland, as well as Yugoslavia. Consequently, the federal government corrected the law on enterprises to eliminate this kind of activity, which could lead to social unrest and demands to stop the reform.

However, I believe that in discussions about the reform process in Yugoslavia, very often too much emphasis is placed on ownership. Certain advocates maintain that the main motivation is private property and private initiative, as the irreplaceable elements for economic efficiency. However, I think it is possible to have public ownership, which is similar to social ownership, of an enterprise, which can be put in the same position as a public enterprise in any market economy.

Furthermore, it is a fact that in modern market economies, a number of larger enterprises, which cover many sectors of production and trade, are corporations: they are incorporated with capital and are not classic private property. Since they sometimes have large numbers of shareholders, they can be treated as social enterprises.

Such an enterprise is not managed by its owner, because there may be thousands of owners, but by professional managers who are skilled and trained for such positions. However, the shareholders can influence the selection of managers, who constitute a separate professional group independent in their management of affairs. Admittance to this group depends mainly on individual skill, training, business acumen and possession of information that translates into astute business decisions. The main criterion for longevity in a management position is the business results at the end of the year, including the rate of profit; these results determine whether a manager can stay or leave. However, the internal structure competes with the managers, whose goal is to minimize the costs to achieve better returns.

Every large enterprise naturally is a system wherein there are several levels of decisionmaking. Of course, it is understandable that all of the employed people cannot make decisions about everything in the enterprise. This was attempted under the self-managing concept, leading to a number of business failures, mismanagement of resources, and inefficient use of capital.

The reform process, now underway throughout the entire socioeconomic system in Yugoslavia, can be completed only if political and economic reforms go hand in hand. The most important thing is to build a consistent rule of law and to stabilize the executive government to ensure a more efficient economy. All of the reforms must consider and legalize equality of the types of ownership: Social, cooperative, private, and mixed. Under this principle, ownerships are not only equal under the law, but they can participate equally in production and trade. There should not be favoritism toward any form of property. World experience shows us that there is no such thing as "monism" ownership, regardless of the ideological prejudices of the different countries.

Therefore, in Yugoslavia, there must not be favored and "protected only" social property, which has had obvious poor results. All forms of ownership must come under the banner of competition, for without competition, we cannot talk about a market economy. Excluding unfair competition places all forms of ownership in competitive positions, where they can show the advantages of entrepreneurship, initiative, and adaptability to modern marketing techniques, to better satisfy needs with existing resources.

Social or government regulation can be justified only if the behavior of enterprises is thereby improved so as to achieve the enterprises' basic goals maximizing profits and reducing costs. The state and government should operate in the most favorable way toward economic units. The different methods used by governments to influence economic life produce different effects in market economies, but generally there is no doubt that government should be responsible for economic growth, stable money, full employment, and balance of payments.

Fiscal and monetary policies are the foundation for the entire economic policy of any country, because these sectors are the main tools government uses to influence economic processes. In almost all market economies with democratic rule, the main issue in election campaigns is usually connected with fiscal and monetary policy. Very often, governments win or lose by their platforms and campaign promises to deliver on it.

In this respect, Yugoslavia has not made enough changes in the reform process, especially to the political system. There is still the conflict of federal sovereignty over sovereignty of the republic, and vice versa. The constitution of 1974 designates that all of the elements of federal macroeconomic policy should be adopted by the federal units and a consensus. Such a regulation causes a long, time-consuming--not to mention complex--procedure, which often totally blocks the system's function. Needless to say, the efficiency of the macroeconomic policy and its influence on the performance of the entire economy is reduced.

11

Sociopolitical Dimensions:
The Market, Political Authority,
and Self-Management
Dusko Sekulic

The classical socialist doctrine proceeds from two premises, which need to be examined and radically redefined if socialism is to have any relevance in light of the changes taking place in contemporary Yugoslav society. These basic premises are the need for planning and the sovereignty of the producer.

PLANNING

Analysis of the nineteenth-century capitalist system of liberal capitalist doctrine led Marx and his successors to two interrelated conclusions. The first was that capitalism is doomed by its inherent nature, through laws on material production that emerge during a particular development phase. Just as capitalism was progressive when it broke away from an outmoded feudal system, so a new system is bound to arise to overcome any obstacles capitalism and its social relationships have left to impede the further development of productive forces. This chapter will not address problems on the collapse of capitalism and the downward trend of profit margins but rather will deal with a second conclusion of the Maxists, drawn from an analysis of trends that they offered as proof that a market economy will not only fail in the long run but is immoral, in that over the short term it makes the rich richer and the poor poorer.

The liberal capitalist economy is under the sovereignty of the capitalists, who determine the quantity of what will be produced. Therefore, the market economy is regulated by the specific needs of a social group, with production targets determined by their wishes. A socialist system would substitute planning for the anarchy of a market economy. A market economy distributes labor and resources according to (ex ante) demand, and that demand is verified on the market (ex post), with unwanted labor and market resources discontinued because the market does not verify the demand for them. On the other hand, the socialist planning system would respond to a differently defined set of requirements. It would have to satisfy the needs defined by organizations of that society, not just the spontaneous needs of consumers or monopolistic corporations. This introduces the new mechanism of planning and new social needs to be met by this implied mechanism.

THE SOVEREIGNTY OF THE PRODUCER

Characteristic of socialist theories and concepts is a concern for the producer, not the consumer. This stems from the historical mission assigned by Marx to the proletariat in the creation of a new system. While the capitalist system exploits direct producers by allowing them to expropriate surplus value, the mission of socialism is to unite the productive function with surplus value management. Hence the owners of capital should no longer determine whether to invest surplus value or distribute it for consumption; rather, these decisions should be made by the producers themselves.

Marxist theories do not analyze the environment of the consumer. For example, when monopoly is discussed, it is criticized for excess profit and possible exploitation from the perspective of a producer, with no analysis of the way that monopoly relates to the consumers. Hence the conceptual approach moves in polar terms, from proprietors or decisionmakers to producers. In fact, a third element, the consumer, is never considered. In reality the system represents a triangle: The decisionmakers, the primary producers, and the consumers. Besides, as individuals, the decisionmakers and producers also have another role as consumers. In order to understand the system, we have to distinguish among these three roles. Marxism neglects the role of the consumer, basing the design of the new system solely on blending the decisionmaker's role with that of the producer, excluding the consumers' role from analysis. This placement of the consumer outside the framework of analysis leads to an approach to economic reform that is blind to the essential contradiction between the producer and the consumer.

SOCIALISM: DECISIONMAKERS, PRODUCERS, AND CONSUMERS

In the classic Marxist version, a combination of the roles of owners and producers resolves the essential issue of whose needs are met by the system (the producer's needs) and the mechanism involved (central planning, which sums up all social needs). In central planning, everything is subordinated to the preferences of those who do the planning. The plan reflects social needs and is implemented through directives. Marx's version, which has never been put into practice anywhere--probably with good reason--the decisionmakers are associated producers. E. Neuberger and W. Duffy wrote about this lack of precision as follows:

> The nature of this decisionmaking structure is not at all clear. The assumption is that there will be a consensus regarding all decisions and aims. With the abolition of the class struggle and with an entire society working as a team, it is not important whether decisions are concentrated at one point or not. Probably there would be a central planning committee, so that the aims would be achieved, but it is not clear how much authority it would have, what the informational structure would be, whether planning would be administrative or manipulative, nor what incentives this committee would give to the producers. The assumption is that everyone would give his labor voluntarily and would receive goods and services according to his needs, irrespective of the quantitative value he had created by his own labor.

Marx probably never even intended to describe in detail what a socialist system should look like. We know he reasoned that the people who could construct this type of system would be sensible enough to make it as good as possible. However, Marx did clearly indicate the basic directions of socialism and communism.

What about the so-called real socialist systems? Apart from the defenders of those systems, every contemporary theoretician of socialism will say that socialism, while abolishing the monopoly of the private proprietor, has introduced another monopoly, called the party center. This is reflected in the economic system as a centrally planned system, responding to the preferences of the planning center, not those of the capitalist or the consumer.

For example, according to Marx, the fundamental relationship between the state and the worker is the identification of state ownership with ownership by the workers' the state is either a workers' collective or under the control of the workers. In other words, it ceases to be a separate and expropriating power. In real countries socialist systems; however, the state becomes a new expropriating power, which a priori represents the interests of the workers through the central planning system to respond to the demands of that expropriating monopolistic center. This means that there is no bonding between producers and decisionmakers; a dispersed decisionmaker (capitalists as a class of owners) has been replaced by a concentrated decisionmaker (the state and its planning center). Accordingly, there is no doubt that the first requirement has been met, in that the real socialist systems are planning systems, different from contemporary capitalist systems, because of their central planning methods. However, the sovereignty of the producers has not been established, although in the ideological version of those representing the system, the state and its planning centers do nothing but represent and plan development to benefit the working class, or producers. Critics of the Stalinist planning model insist that such planning is calculated to strengthen the new ruling class and maintain the staus quo.

The preceding conceptual analysis provides us with an avenue of escape from the crisis in contemporary socialist systems. The overall assessment suggests that their economic performance has been far from optimal, and they have made obvious attempts to modify the classic system of central planning. The Yugoslav system, for one, is in crisis. In fact, some of the solutions offered are not far removed from those characteristic of real socialism. A solution to the crisis emerges from the above analysis, leading in several directions:

1. The basic view is that the system of central planning, as it evolved in real socialist systems, is to blame for economic problems, and that the introduction of market forces will help restore efficiency.

2. The principal blame for the inefficient system must rest squarely on the lack of sovereignty of the producers. The planning center (the state and the party) dominates, which means that a viable solution to the crisis may be replacement of the party-state planning center by giving sovereignty to the producers.

3. A combination of these two approaches is possible through the market by giving a greater role to the producers, taking one of two fundamental approaches. One of these is closer to the classical Marxist analysis, which disregards the consumer's role; the other takes a different look at the producer.

CULPABILITY OF THE CENTRALIST SYSTEM

Most of the current reforms in real socialist countries evolved from the idea that the centrally planned system is too rigid to give optimal results at the contemporary level in the development of productive forces. It is noted that the phrase, "at the contemporary level in the development of productive forces," provides the creators of the system with an escape route, for such a centrally planned system can only be created in the future, because the climate is not yet ready for it.

More radical critics wonder if this planning system is feasible for any kind of regulation, especially in the highly developed societies of the future, although applications to the past can be made with interesting results. For example, was the New Economic Policy (NEP) a retreat or a step forward? Was the consistent Stalinist implementation of the planning system near the end of the 1920s a return to the true path or a moratorium on new forms of exploration?

A measure of market regulation at the expense of central planning has been into these systems, with Hungary and China presently in the forefront, although it once was Yugoslavia that took the lead in these experiments. If the allocative function of the market or the development of a system based on consumer preferences as expressed in the market is acknowledged, then the consumer is introduced into the game, even in socialist countries. Sectors producing consumer goods usually are the first to succumb to the market mechanism, with the consumer playing a direct role. Those sectors producing investment goods remain within the realm of direct control much longer.

What really is happening here? Obviously, the planning function of the state is weakened, being replaced not by the planning function of the producer, but rather by the sovereignty of the consumer (the market), which is combined with the considerable influence of the state. What about the producers and their sovereignty? They do not acquire sovereignty in Marx's sense, because they do not govern the operation of the system as a whole. Sovereignty passes from the planners to the consumers as the market functions. However, in this system, the consumers do not acquire sovereignty, but autonomy. Sovereignty means that the system is dependent on the decisions of the individual, who has the power to force others to act on his preferences. In the plan system, sovereignty is centralized in the planning center, while market-system sovereignty is dispersed among the consumers. In a market system the producers (firms) acquire autonomy and make decisions not only to satisfy the consumers but also to sustain this autonomy, being subjected up front to decisions built into the plan.

To those representing Marxist orthodoxy, this solution looks like either a temporary retreat, with the consoling thought that either the productive forces are not yet ready for the plan system or that there has been possibly a betrayal of certain basic principles because the planning function is weakened. Marx believed it to be vital that that ex ante regulation replace ex post regulation; in an anarchic market, producer sovereignty is also replaced by autonomy.

CULPABILITY OF AN UNDEMOCRATIC SYSTEM

Planning cannot be blamed in this interpretation, although it is inherent in socialism to blame. Abuse of planning by a bureaucratic management caused the crisis, and the sovereignty of the planning center in governing development must be replaced by the sovereignty of the working class. Here we have planning and producers, but we do not have the consumers or the market. This train of thought is based on depriving the bureaucratic center of its power and replacing its sovereignty with the sovereignty of the producers.

A system of this kind is most often put into

practice through a council in which the decisionmaking process operates from the bottom up. For example, the framework of this plan would not be based on decisions made at the center but rather on agreements with all of the producers and firms. Thus, the latter would have acquired sovereignty and the system would conform to their directives, although they would not have autonomy. In such a system there would be an agreement by the producers giving the firms equal voice in planning targets. They would have no autonomy in the implementation process, because collective decisions would be implemented. We might call such a system a model of democratic centralism, because it arrives at economic decisions in a way that would replace the centralism of contemporary real socialist planned economies.

The theoretical concept of self-management is discussed for the first time in detail by A. Gramsci, who writes that under self-management the state is a centralized, hierarchical pyramid of workers' councils organized on production lines. The state regulates both economic planning and legislative activity, with political authority radiating from the workers' councils, which perform the task formerly fulfilled by the capitalists. The nonproductive supervisory functions vanish, but the expert managerial functions remain. Hence, an egalitarian entity is incorporated, to produce goods through a cooperative production process, which means that the state is not organized on a territorial but rather on a production principle.

The essential consideration here is that since the authority of the workers' councils must replace the economic power of the capitalists, decisions by the workers' councils must eliminate the competitive market on a higher level. Shares allotted to production, expenditures, and investments are not determined by the market but rather by the central decisions of democratically elected workers' councils. Therefore, economic decisions are not controlled by the market or by different types of consumers with various needs and demands, but through a political process of agreement, with decisions arrived at democratically to reflect the opinions of the producers, not the consumers, about what constitutes "socially useful" production, according to Gramsci's terminology.

In order to clarify these arguments, I would like to quote certain authors more extensively, to present the similarity of their approach. According to Maurice H. Dobb, in a bureaucratic and centralized economy with central authorities, some organ of central government, arbitrarily determines the investment levels, from which issues the actual volume of consumption. Sacrifices are again imposed without regard for those affected and without their prior consent. A system of management like this is contrary to the principles of socialism, for it leads to lower economic performance than is present in a democratic system of management. It confers the power to dispose of the social surplus of production to the central political, economic, and military administration, giving the administration the power to control and subject all of society to its authority. In non-Marxist terms, what the Communist Party of the Soviet Union designated as the excessive cult of personality is nothing more than the ultimate conclusion of an arbitrary exercise of bureaucratic power over the economy and society as a whole.

The revolution which socialism brings about in the economic and social structure presumes that the masses, in their own interests, will be bound by the decision to devote part of the available resources to potential current expenditure and the development of productive forces. As opposed to capitalism or a system of bureaucratic planning, this decision becomes a "freely accepted sacrifice."

On a long-term basis, socialist democracy makes possible more harmonious and rapid growth of the economy than does bureaucratic planning.

I believe that this quotation graphically presents the argument I put forth at the beginning of this section. The negative aspects of the system arise when a single center plans development in an undemocratic fashion and, in turn, demands sacrifices and the renunciation of the present level of consumption to build for the future, although the individuals required to make the sacrifice have not given their consent voluntarily. This is not socialism; under socialism, people consent freely and decide on the volume and allocation of the investment. Apart from the moral judgments that this is not socialism, if the influence of the masses and socialist democracy are lacking in economic development, there is also the argument of efficiency. The present system is less efficient because it is undemocratic; it must be democratized, and decisionmaking at the center must be replaced by democratic decisionmaking by all; this will improve the efficiency of the system.

K. Mihajlovic applies the same idea to Yugoslavia

that overall priorities should be based on democratic discussion, with the underlying tone determined by the working class, which is historically destined to govern not only economic relationships in production and working conditions, but all walks of life, for the satisfaction of genuine human needs.

The working class has never been in a position to freely prioritize its needs; consequently, there is no basis for knowing how it will react in such an environment. Considering its historical mission and responsibilities, guidelines would already be in place to abolish discrimination and privileges but satisfy genuine human needs not based on prestige. For the young and largely peasant working class, priorities would be set for (1) employment because of the mass migration of labor (7 million people) into the cities after the war, (2) housing construction, (3) increased food supply, and (4) improvement of working conditions, health, education, and other aspects of communal consumption. It is not probable that there would be the resources to build everyone a weekend cottage or enough production to create conditions that would broaden social differences.

This is the same argument that E. Mandel (1970) applies to Yugoslavia. It transpires from Mihajlovic"s analysis above that central decisionmaking, which is inherently undemocratic, made wrong strategic decisions that led to a series of anomalies and distortions in economic and social development. If the working class had made democratic decisions on development priorities, such anomalies would not have surfaced. At the same time, Mihajlovic holds that the present difficulties could be blamed on the market's uncontrolled activities, resulting from of certain central decisions that had been arrived at through a democratic mechanism for decisionmaking and assigning priorities.

We can find a description of this mechanism in the work of P. Vranicki (1985, pp. 174-80). He accurately discusses Gramsci's ideas and gives them concrete form for our use. Only when a self-management organization exists that is competent to manage on a daily basis can we speak to the possibility of the working class governing a wide range of productive operations and the principal economic processes. The creation of workers' councils on that productive and functional line, from the commune up to the republic and federation, would make it possible for the associations of workers to manage these processes. I think the existing associated labor committees could address the basic issues of large-scale production and self-management planning would be settled.

The working class--the producers in the factories and farms--must be so organized in self-management that it establishes its sovereign rights in its own working processes, from the lowest level to the highest, federal, level. I think the most logical and most effective self-management organizational style for the working class would be an organization of workers' councils drawn from the various branches of production or larger productive units; these councils being composed of basic organizations of associated labor through municipal, district, republic, and federal councils. Together, all of the worker's councils of the municipality, the district, the republic, and the federation form committees of associated labor at each given level for mutual cooperation, association, and exchanges among individual producers. The activities of all of these councils would mean that the search was on for large-scale production governed by the working class.

If this kind of working-class decisionmaking were translated into entirely concrete terms, it would mean that producers in the metal, textile, and other specific branches of industrial production, or in any major productive unit, would select delegates to the worker's council of the metalworkers, textile operatives, and so on, at the municipality level; in associations of municipalities, districts, or republics; or at the level of the federation. At each social level, these councils would resolve all of the essential issues of development and function of specific branches of production. All of the councils would form at each level a committee of associated labor to deal with the development of the economy and investment proposals for its own region. This would be confirmed with other committees at the republic and federal levels as the overall plan of the republic and the federation.

DIAGNOSING THE CRISIS

Identifying the basic dilemma in the crisis in Yugoslav society and socialism yields possible solutions. Proceeding from the accepted fact that planning is a good thing in socialist societies, the central planning model properly belongs in the arsenal of instruments to regulate the economic mechanism. What is "bad" and what induces the crisis is not so much the mechanism of central planning itself, but that a government conducted in an undemocratic way attempts to implement this mechanism through a small group of individuals, without consulting the people. The prescription for a cure to this problem lies in the democratization of the planning mechanism, not only to allow for responses to suggestions from the top but also to serve a broad segment of society. Since the directive from above is the main instrument of the planned economy, it would remain, but only in a democratic fashion, whereas in contemporary real socialist systems, it issues from an undemocratic decisionmaking procedure. Maximum attention, then, must be focused on the construction of democratic machinery, as discussed by Vranicki.

However, a diagnosis emphasizing the defects of a centralized planning mechanism offers a different prescription. It proceeds from the assumption that this system must be dismantled and replaced by a more market-oriented economy. Emphasis is on the dismantling of the central planning system, not on its democratization. The reasoning is that if a centralized system is to blame for the inefficiency, then democratization will not essentially change the economic performance of the system. Since democracy in planning, formulation of decisions, and regulation of the economy is not to be construed as democracy in the classic political sense, democratization of the planning mechanism would not in essence change its nature and performance. If we operate a centrally planned economy by agreement, its performance will be about the same whether the an economy whether the planning is based on democratic decisions made by a council or on the same kind of decisionmaking as in other centralized systems. Of course, the statement that its performance will be more or less the same is valid only on an ideal typical level, where our analysis is in any case pitched. Probably there would be shifts in targets, although I do not share the optimism of the passage from Mihajlovic, for I do not know what it was based on, apart from the faith that the goals of workers in a dialogue would be different from the goals of top bureaucracy. Whether those aims would be better is another matter, since people are inclined to implement decisions they have participated in more wholeheartedly than they implement decisions that have been imposed on them. Would this system remain less efficient than a system based on market mechanisms?

The fate of our reforms lies precisely in this oscillation. When a move is made to dismantle the central system, to begin the construction of a market economy, and to exercise the beneficial effects of relieving production firms from state authority and pressure for political democracy, then we have taken a step backwards. However, this process has its ideological disguise, which leaves ostensible room for actual reforms. This means that the market economy is actually relinquished at the expense of democracy in the central planning mechanism. In an attempt to retain a planned, but democratic, economy, the economic reforms of 1965 produced an economy based on agreements, as the most detailed system of abandonment of a market economy in an attempt to retain a planned, but democratic, economy. The failure of the long-term program of economic stabilization will probably produce new theoretical ideas and a new economy based on agreements. This pressure for an agreement economy is simple, because it makes inviolate the basic postulates of socialism. One of these is a planned society, which always makes socialists feel ill at ease when faced with the spontaneous operation of the market. The second postulate is the domination of the producers or the working class.

An agreement economy is planned to ensure the domination of the working class, because consumers and the market are not essential categories. In an example of the nostalgia for democratic planning, which has never been implemented in a centrally planned system, there is an interesting work by Dz. Sokolovic (1986), according to whom, while the production of commodities develops the rational organization of the work process, it simultaneously inhibits the development of another element-- production by need.

The climax of this paradoxical effect of commodity production or of the market on work may be expressed in these words: The more a work-oriented society develops, the less that work becomes social. While producing more and more for the market, a man produces more and more for others, which is the social nature of work, but he produces less for their needs and less in concrete terms. Commodity production develops the social nature of work within alienation. To produce in a social manner in an authentic sense does not simply mean to produce for other people; to produce for man means to produce for his needs.

According to Sokolovic, the market does not produce for proper human needs. Only a planned economy can be organized to meet such needs. At the same time, a

156

mechanism must exist to transmit impluses from the needs to the economic system, which has to know what to produce and how to produce it to satisfy these needs. Abstracting for the moment from any discussion about "right" or "wrong" needs, which is somewhat metaphysical, it remains to be confirmed that both the market and the plan--irreconcilable forms of regulation--are specific mechanisms for satisfying needs.

In an ideal sense, the consumers in a market system are those whose preferences are satisfied by the system. In a centrally planned system, the system satisfies the preferences of the planning center. Modification or democratization of the central planning system would not change this essential feature, because of the democratic decisionmaking mechanism, it would be the needs of the organized producers that would be satisfied. Thus the actors who control the behavior of the system are (1) the consumers, (2) the planning center, and (3) the organized producers. Prior repudiation of the possibility that the market system could respond to the needs of the people is tantamount to saying that people are not aware of their true needs, but that there must be a planning center to control production to satisfy those needs. This line of thought has its tradition in classical Marxism, where historical interests are distinguished from empirical interests --an analogy of "warped" and "true" needs.

The idea that the planning mechanism represents the chief instrument of socialism may be found in Lenin.

For socialism is no more than the first step forward from the monopoly of state capitalism. Or, in other words, socialism is nothing but the monopoly of state capitalism turned to the advantage of the entire nation, which has to that extent ceased to be a capitalist monopoly.

These words contain the diagnosis of the crisis. The "mistake" does not lie in the state monopoly through the practice of the central planning mechanism but rather in that this monopoly is not a "proper" socialist monopoly. The thesis of "market" socialism is that any monopoly has to be destroyed, because a bureaucratic monopoly has the same effect as a monopoly by the producers, which must be replaced by a market system with a consumer monopoly. In a market system there is no monopoly, but a decentralized influence on the producers.

The principal task of the market theory of

socialism derived from this, is to shatter the complacency of classical Marxists, who believe the main problem to be the establishment of a monopoly of producers. In Marxism, the problem is how to remove decisionmaking power from the hands of capitalists and give it to producers, while contemporary theorists in socialist countries ponder how to take the power from the hands of bureaucrats and give it to producers. Market socialism insists on breaking any monopoly, including the potential monopoly of producers, the economy, and the working class or associated labor. It is not vital that the working class control large-scale production; as Vranicki says, it has been established at all levels of our society that the fundamental reason for these distortions is that the working class still does not have control over the surplus from work or large-scale production. Of vital importance is (1) how to break the monopoly of any party or working class; (2) how to install a system with a mechanism capable of directly responding to human needs through a market system; and (3) how to include in that mechanism corrective and allocative democratic controls.

CONSUMER PREFERENCES

It is not my intent to delve deeply into the intricacies of the market function mechanism, although the evolution in attitudes about market mechanisms needs to be addressed.

The sociological context of the classical Marxist doctrine has been stressed, with the problem being that producers do not play a majority role. The owners (private owners in the classical sense or the state in contemporary analyses) are not ignored, while the consumers receive tacit understanding.

Marxist-inspired contemporary analysis cannot ignore this problem, although it offers its own simple solutions. Consumers do exist, although with diminishing marginal influence, flavored with the economic development of capitalism.

A non-Marxist classical view of this attitude is presented by the influential left-wing liberal John Galbraith.

The time has now come to promulgate as a firm conclusion something which up until now we have simply kept announcing. How economic resources-- capital, labor, and materials--will be allocated for production and how they will be used in the private and state sectors of industry depends on the power of the producers. The more an economy develops, the greater this dependence. This is one of the fundamental tendencies of an economic system. In the neo-classical model, consumers and citizens have control of production, and they exercise it by their choice of what to buy. The balance which emerges is co-ordinated with their needs, as they themselves interpret them and fulfill them through their income. However, in contemporary reality, this balance is simply a reflection of the power of the producers; the latter, the power of the producers, not needs, is what determines what an economy will do.

Hence, if this diagnosis is correct, there is no point in insisting on the introduction of a market system, because it will not lead to consumer control. More subtly, if market systems are dominated by the producers, then the introduction of a market system would mean eliminiation of the bureaucratic monopoly and the establishment of a producers' monopoly, which would be exactly what socialist theorists want. But the reason this argument is not pursued is that the domination Galbraith is referring to is actually an uncoordinated domination by individual segments. The segments are linked in different ways to the state through the control of system operations. The ideal is that all producers should influence the system in the same way, promoting a new democracy to steer economic development democracy based on the role individuals play in the production process. The authors cited in this chapter accept this thesis, but there is the attitude that consumer preferences do not carry weight, with control by "sensible" producers, instead of by the incompetent bureaucrats who had prior control.

Mihajlovic advances his conclusion:

The arguments and views advanced repudiate a more significant role for the consumer in determining a priority of needs. When it is left to the market to regulate economic relationships, Yugoslav experience has confirmed that the decisive role in determining the priority and development of needs properly belongs to the production sector.

The defect in this solution is that production as a means has presumed to define ends whose definition imitates a consumer society. It is crucial to grasp the essential difference between the mission of production which creates income, and production which not only creates income but serves to satisfy human needs in the best possible manner. It makes a great deal of difference whether production is worthwhile and socially sensible.

Mihajlovic points to certain consumer preferences which have been influenced by Western patterns of consumption. Although consumers have no influence on trends in productive development, they are the willing objects of manipulation. He also blames consumers for having created a consumer mentality, even in low-income groups, buying cars instead of living accommodations and going on holidays and excursions abroad for prestige, not from actual need.

I do not think that we in Yugoslavia have become captivated by this consumer mentality, nor do I believe that we possess the right tools to evaluate our actual needs. Travel abroad isjust as proper a need as others; only question is whether there is wealth to satisfy such needs. As affluence increases there will be more travel abroad, and as educational standards rise, these trips will not be only a consumption, but will but possess content as well. Where there is a struggle for accommodations, ownership of cars rather than apartments or houses is entirely rational, because purchasing is difficult, while cars are readily available. I entirely agree that the choice of priorities is to blame. But the problems are not confined because "domestic production has become an extension of production for profit and its manipulation by demand. As far as many items of personal consumption in Yugoslavia are concerned, the deciding factor is foreign production, which creates and imposes on us fashionable inventions and inessential novelties."

Nevertheless, I would be prepared to trust people, as consumers, to judge for themselves what their needs are. Personal consumption might be on a much higher level of consumer satisfaction if foreign production criteria were present to an even greater degree. I do not believe the solution is to grant a monopoly to the producers instead of to a bureaucracy--after all, Mihajlovic also criticizes the producers for having become extensions of production for profit. I do not think the problem can be solved by creating integrated control over the

160

economy on a council basis, as in Vranicki's model, either. Rather, I see the solution in increased consumer influence. If the economy were more market-oriented, there would probably be more apartments available, not fewer. Fewer apartments are the result of misguided bureaucratic policy, based on the premise of proper needs or the belief that people should be given apartments without earning them. A strategy to abolish these assumptions, with the introduction of a consistent market--and not a new monopolistic center for decisionmaking--would help to relieve the crisis.

This is based on the assumption that extreme points of view are not correct. It is not entirely correct for consumers to determine production in an ideal sense; nor is it correct, as Galbraith claims, for producers to determine what will be produced. Galbraith believes that over the long term, society will discover new mechanisms to control economic growth. Liberal capitalism has long since yielded to regulated capitalism. But this long-term tendency does mean that the regulative mechanisms of the market and the sovereignty of the consumer are abolished. They still operate within limits, and even though they are regulated, they are still effective. A concise analysis may be found in O. Sik (1983, pp. 173-74), who avoids extremes. There are both monopolies and producer influences in the existing market economies, but to a degree the pressure of the market is always exerted on both monopolies and producers.

Thus, Sik attributes to Galbraith a claim that the technostructure constantly tries to make the activities of commercial firms conform to its own aims and that large firms attempt to make society's aims conform to the aims of the technostructure. However, given market conditions, both sets of objectives are conditioned objectively. Even in a partial market, this pattern is followed when (1) production in these structures evolves to levels corresponding to real demands, as determined by the method of distribution; (2) production develops in concert with the active exploitation of productive factors, leading to a qualitative development of the market and an increase in productivity; and (3) production increases serviceable values--their quality enhanced--and creation of the new products necessary to society.

Theoretically, in capitalist systems the regulator is the market (the consumers), and in socialist systems the regulator is the planning center (the

161

plan). In actual practice, however, there is a wide difference from these models. Consumers alone do not determine production in market systems; there are monopolies, domination by the producer through advertising, and an ever-increasing state influence. Planning centers do not have sole control over production in the planning system, either; certain sectors are not subject to the plan, and besides the formal influence by producers, there is indirect consumer influence through a quasi-market, and there are economic reforms directed toward a deliberate emancipation of the market.

However, the basic difference between the two systems remains. Although certain authors, Galbraith for one, proclaim convergencies between the systems, there still remain certain basic differences. Economically, the difference involves the determinant for systems operation. Any reforms must proceed along a path leading to the creation of market socialism; that is, socialism must venture forth on a completely different road.

If we abandon planning as the essence of socialism, and if the producers, who are supposed to control this planning, no longer dominate, what is left of socialism? Is this not simply an acknowledgment that socialism is an economically unsuccessful system, and that we should liquidate the existing socialist countries by turning them into capitalist countries through peaceful means? Orthodox Marxists threaten this whenever any of the socialist countries begin to implement market-model reforms.

Reforms in socialism should serve as a hypothesis for a way out of the current crisis, proceeding with the recognition that the utopian ideal of overall planning and the control of production, whether by a bureaucratic center or associated producers, is incapable of blending with the real trends and demands of economic life. As long as there is a shortage there must be an economy, dedicated to extracting the maximum from limited resources. The commodity aspect of the economy, combined with various forms of regulation, must be the main determinant of the economic process. When the preconditions for a communist society are created, wrote M. Korac at the end of his massive book (1977),

it is not unrealistic to expect that further development of science and industry in a socialist self-management society will permit the conversion, not only of human speech but also of thoughts, into active energy, and that it will be possible for production and other forms of technology to generate all of the material goods people require, not only through oral instructions or even by the anticipation of their wishes or registration of their thoughts.

It is certain that the development of productive forces on this level can be achieved only through the efforts of people who have been prepared by socialist self-management commodity production for the communist mode of noncommodity production, or for life and work in a truly human communist community. Only such individuals will be able to benefit from this developed mode of production and for those other forms of technology which make it possible for their words or thoughts to be converted directly into actions or material goods, so the human race may at last be free of the necessity to slave in the interests of material production; then the need for a commodity economy will also lapse.

Economic model reforms must follow a different path for the future, through (1) abandonment of a rigid bureaucratic planning structure for the economy; (2) introduction of autonomy for economic subjects; and (3) a market mechanism for trading. Sik states in his theoretical study (1983) the direction economic reforms socialism should take.

If the market mechanism is to continue functioning to its fullest extent, planning must not be permitted to embrace production and investment activity. Enterprises must continue to control their production and their investment development on the basis of their own responsibility. Aims adopted in the plan may be realized with the help of certain distributive processes through the allocation of gross income or the gross national income to certain income groups. This development may again be achieved through a suitable economic policy.

Silk's orientation is toward a market economy in a limited private sector--less than in the socialist countries at present, with indirect macro-regulation and democratically determined goals.

The goals of economic reforms must include (1) the reallocation of authority within the planning system to strengthen the producer, (2) a restructuring of the entire planning system, and (3) the creation of a model for market socialism. Proposals on the various planning mechanisms of a council, or the popular term "agreement economy," merely distract from the reforms that must follow to ensure long-term recovery in socialist economies.

SUMMARY

There are two basic diagnoses of what is wrong with the contemporary economic mechanisms of socialist systems. One diagnosis proclaims planning as the basic component of socialism. The crisis in this view is not the result of the planning itself but rather of the undemocratic planning process. The second diagnosis criticizes the whole idea of planning and develops the idea of market socialism. From these two judgements, two strategies develop. One is oriented to the democratization of the centrally planned system (council democracy) and the other toward market replacement of planning mechanisms. In an orthodox view, nothing is wrong with the idea of a monopoly inherent in central planning philosophy. In market-oriented thinking, every monopoly is bad regardless of whether it is controlled by the private owner, the state, or organized producers. Consumers should recognize their role no matter how imperfect their influence may be in practice.

12

Reform in 1990:
The Shift to a Mixed Economy
Aleksandra Jovanovic

For an understanding of the significance and scope of reform in Yugoslavia in 1990, a brief overview must be presented of the defects in the Yugoslav economy, which pertains to the ownership rights structure and its influence on the behavior of the Yugoslav firm. The impact of the ownership rights structure on the behavior of the firm is examined because all empirical data support the almost unanimous opinion of economists that the Yugoslav institutional setting contained negative incentives, so that its economic inefficiency can be attributed mainly to the system of social ownership. An examination must also be made of the provisions of the reform laws, which relate directly or indirectly to the regulation of ownership rights and therefore to the behavior of the firm, must be made.

Since 1952 the declared institutional foundation of the system has been self-management as the dominant production mode for social ownership, and a mixture of planning and marketing to coordinate economic activity. These major institutional principles, which were declared in the constitution and other acts, remained stable until 1990, although operational changes were made at times to improve the efficiency of the system. The need for these operational reforms proved not only that the constitutional definition of the system was different from the economic reality, but that the economic system should be institutionally changed.

In focusing on the evolutionary behavior of the Yugoslav firm, we see changes in the regulatory constraints under which Yugoslav firms operated. These regulatory constraints were imposed through rules of distribution of a firm's income to make the social ownership principle concrete. These rules were needed because of the virtual absence of a capital and labor market.

The evolution of distribution rules can be depicted in two major phases: the first was the 1965--71 reform, and the second phase was called the "agreement economy," and began in 1971. The common characteristic of both phases was the use of the concept of income. In the Yugoslav economy this concept is understood quite differently from the way it usually is, because income is understood as revenue, from which depreciation and the costs of raw materials are deducted. Since wages are part of net income, they are not considered a cost.

The 1965 reform introduced the concept of income as the crucial category of the Yugoslav economy, and the 1968 law on distribution of income made the whole institutional setting rely on the category of income. At the same time, this was a period of decentralization in the Yugoslav economy, in which a certain autonomy was given to the firms. Workers' collectives were allowed to make decisions about the proportions of personal income (wages) and accumulation in income. This meant that workers' collectives decided the price of capital and labor.

Although without constraints in the disposition of income, the accumulation and personal income proportion data suggested consistency across the economy, in that (1) the share of accumulation in the income of the firm was the increasing function of income per worker compared with the average in the economy, and (2) the share of personal income was a decreasing function of income per worker (compared with the average in the economy) if the firm's income per worker was larger than the average economic income per worker.

When constraints were not imposed on workers' collective decisionmaking about capital and labor price levels, the objective function of the Yugoslav firm was income per worker:

$$y = pQ/L$$

pQ is understood as income (revenue net from depreciation and costs of raw materials)

The maximization result, according to the well-known properties of the neoclassical short-term production function, is:

$$Q1' = Q/L \text{ and } Qk' = 0$$

This means that the incremental employment of labor reaches a level in which the marginal product of labor is equalized with the average product. If not, the value of the marginal product of labor reaches the level of income per worker, and the equilibrium use of capital will reach such a level that the marginal product of capital is zero.

Although this model excluded the price of capital, workers' collectives could separate that part of income in the accumulation fund. The absence of capital and labor markets meant that factor prices were determined by the workers' collectives. The Yugoslav system did not recognize the price of capital except in a few cases involving planned expenditures and long-range decisionmaking. However, although the price of capital was not formally recognized, that price did exist and consisted of (1) depreciation and the interest rate of loans, if the firm were externally financed, and (2) the accumulation rate, if the firm were internally financed. Being determined from hindsight when the workers' collective decided on the distribution of income, the factor-price level could only work out its allocation and distribution function by chance. In this way, the factor prices were pseudo-prices, which simulated market determination of prices without market rationality.

After 1971 distribution of income was regulated by "social agreements," which imposed distribution rules according to the above spontaneously established proportions to form factor prices. The imposition of these rules meant that the government needed to protect social capital accumulation.

The "agreement economy" was continued in the next phase, which began in 1976 with the enactment of the Law on Associated Labor. This law determined income distribution only on a principle basis, by proclaiming (1) that personal income (wages) was dependent on the contribution of labor to production and to management and (2) that accumulation was dependent on the industry the firm was engaged in. The application of these principles was left to "social agreements."

The common characteristic of this type of legislature (the Law on Associated Labor and "social agreements" based on this law) was that it tied the distribution of income in the firm to the relationship of (1) income per worker in the firm and (2) the economic average income per worker. If income per worker in the firm were higher than the economic average income per worker, the accumulation rate in the firm should be relatively higher than the economic average accumulation rate. Personal income could also be higher than the average economic personal income. On the other hand, if the firm's income per worker were less than the average in the economy, then its accumulation could be less than the average accumulation. However, personal income could also be less than the average personal income in the economy. These rules impacted on the objective function and behavior of the Yugoslav firm.

Expressing these constraints in the income distribution function (b) in the internally financed firm are:

$$b = b (Z, ym) Z$$ where: b = income distribution function
Z = net income per worker
Z = pQ/L
ym = exogenously determined (average) personal income (wage) in the economy

The aim function (y) of the firm, considering the constraints imposed by the income distribution function (b), was the function that maximized the share of wages (y) in income per worker (Z):

$$y = b (Z, ym) Z$$

Following the agreement rule that income per worker in the firm (Z) must be larger than the economic average income per worker (Zm), if the wages are larger than the economic average wages, the maximization condition can be written as:

$$y = b (Z, ym) Z > b (Zm, ym) Zm = ym$$

Under the given condition, the rate of accumulation (a) was:

$$a = (1 - b) pQ/K$$

The results obtained from this model (maximization of income per worker) are the same as in the preceding model without constraints. The only difference is that in the model in which constraints were imposed, workers could not use the whole income as personal income (wages). The constraints made accumulation obligatory.

The approach to the creation of the aim function

through regulation of the distribution of income did not include income-per-worker dependency on capital intensity. This meant that the rule of distribution could be obeyed even though the share of accumulation was not appropriate to the contribution of capital to income and that workers would acquire more than the amount of the labor contribution. This distortion in factor prices was dangerous not only for volume accumulation but also for factor allocation.

In 1985 the new social agreement phase began to determine the distribution of income and factor prices. The rate of accumulation and the wage rate were somewhat dependent on the relationship of income per worker, plus income per average use of capital in the firm, with economic average income per worker, plus income per use of capital. The new constraint was introduced in order to avoid the problems of the previous model, which made it possible to obey the rule but not make a real factor-price evaluation.

The new constraint consisted of the following three cumulative conditions in which income per worker in the firm had to be higher than the economic average income per worker:

1. Income per use of capital in the firm had to be higher than the economic average income per use of capital;

2. The rate of accumulation in the firm had to be higher than the economic average rate of accumulation; and

3. This had to be satisfied to increase the wages in the firm over the level of the economic average wages.

With this constraint, labor income became the function of the rate of accumulation. A rigorous mathematical explanation of the model would be too lengthy for this chapter; but it would show that this constraint established an unusual correlation between the rate of accumulation and wages. This function excludes both the conflict of economic interests in distribution and the trade-off between wages and the rate of accumulation.

In looking at the behavior of the firm and the institutional setting imposed by the 1990 legislature, especially changes in the ownership right structure, three reform laws stand out: (1) the Enterprises Law (Sluzbeni list SFRJ, nos. 77/88, 40/89, 16/90); (2) the Social Capital Law (Sluzbeni list SFRJ, nos. 84/89, 46/90); and (3) the Law on personal Income Payments (Sluzbeni list SFRJ, no. 37/90).

The first step toward a mixed economy was the enactment of the Enterprises Law, which had provisions that declared the equality of the various types of ownership. All enterprises have the same status, rights, and responsibilities regardless of their ownership-right structure, which may be private, social, cooperative, or mixed. Self-management remains the basic principle in socially owned firms, and in the socially owned part of the firms with mixed ownership. In firms with other types of ownership, workers can participate in management in conformity with collective contracts.

The Yugoslav economy changed its nature. Self-management remained the decisionmaking principle only in that segment of the economy that operates under social ownership rules. Even there, more discrete authority is given to the managers on layoffs and wages. Self-management has been adjusted to the new form of market competition.

Recognizing the well-known efficiency of private ownership, attention is focused on the socially owned enterprises and how their behavior has changed in the new institutional setting. First, the socially owned sector is the dominant one in Yugoslavia, although this casts doubt on the declared equality status of various types of ownership. One should bear in mind that denoted laws provide an opportunity for gradual changes from social ownership into other types of property. The equality of various types of ownership is important to establish competition and to improve the efficiency of the remaining social sector.

Second, it is not clear whether a new institutional setting will have an impact on the objective function of the socially owned firm. The Enterprise Law defines profit or income as objective function. Profit as objective function pertains to private firms, but determining income as the objective function of the socially owned firm is imprecise and not adequate to reality. From the preceding historical overview, we saw that the objective function of the Yugoslav firm, although changing at times, was always a mechanism for maximizing labor income, and that this objective function did not necessarily cause the firms to operate more efficiently. This resulted from the way factor prices were determined, not as parameters for the firms but rather as decisionmaking variables. According to Enterprise Law provisions, the concept

170

of income has remained as a natural consequence of the unchanged concept of social ownership. In the institutional setting, where the process of privatization of the firms changes the income distribution on the firm's level and where self-management is geared to perform adequately within the market framework without factor markets, the objective function of a socially owned firm has become vague. The mix of the two concepts, profit and income, reflects the blending of different ownership segments in the Yugoslav economy.

Third, the Enterprise Law holds the promise of a reorganization of socially owned enterprises as joint stock companies. Using shares instead of debts for additional capital-raising finance is something new. The right of one socially owned firm to acquire the proceeds from the ownership of shares in another socially owned firm means that social ownership rights have become a formal basis for acquisitions.

The Social Capital Law goes one step further, by allowing transition of social into private ownership. This law regulates the procurement of additional capital by issuing shares or selling socially owned enterprises, or by selling the interest of the enterprise. The funds raised through additional investment belong to the enterprise. The enterprise and social capital may be sold as a whole or in part to any domestic or foreign legal entity or natural person. In this case, the proceeds from the sale of the enterprise (whole or part) belong to the Development Fund, which operates as a public enterprise, using the proceeds for investment in the enterprise or for other purposes. The proceeds represent the interest of the republic or the autonomous province; the fund represents the role of the state in controlling the privatization process and the formation of state ownership.

If an enterprise issues shares or sells interest in the enterprise or sells social capital as a part of the enterprise, it must be reorganized as one of mixed ownership.

In the absence of a capital market, the transformation of social capital is a difficult endeavor, although the capital market and money market are regulated by one of the 1990 reform laws. The law gives authorization to the Development Fund to determine the institution, which issues shares and sells capital and states the rules for estimating the value of social capital.

The Law on Personal Income Payments makes issuing shares or bonds obligatory to workers in socially owned firms if the index of calculated personal income per worker in the firm is more than 90 percent compared with the economic average of personal income from December 1989 to May 1990. The issue of shares relates to the amount of increase in personal income of the firm.

The general principle of transforming social ownership into private ownership is not questioned. In order to make the economy efficient, self-management rights should be connected to ownership rights. Although the general principle is not in question, there are doubts about the provision of obligatory shares for the workers instead of an increase in personal income. This administrative control in determining personal income has provoked discussion and dispute, because it reduces the autonomy of the firms.

Through the 1990 reform, the Yugoslav economy obtained a necessary, but insufficient, legal basis to change the cumbersome economic system. This was the legal mandate for changes in fundamental principles in order to make the transformation from a self-managed economy to a mixed economy.

III

European Integration

13

Yugoslavia in Europe:
Economic and Political Integration
Rikard Stajner

Yugoslavia is in the heart of Europe and thus occupies a geopolitical location between Western and Eastern and between Southern and Central Europe. Because of this, there is a fateful link between developments in Europe and Yugoslavia. Not so long ago the Sarajevo assassination, which was committed in the name of a libertarian movement, brought on World War I and ushered in the postwar libertarian movement in Europe.

In World War II, Yugoslavia, with the fourth-strongest Allied military force, was the only European country occupied by Fascist forces in which large areas of liberated territory were controlled by resistance forces and an army of its citizens successfully fought on the side of the Allies. The occupation left a deep gash on recent European civilization.

By resisting Stalin after the war, Yugoslavia was able to pursue a policy of independence, initial market-oriented reforms, democratization of the system, and openness to Europe and the world. This policy displayed an early anticipation of the events to come in European socialist countries; its foresight is now evident.

Economically, Yugoslavia is primarily connected with European countries, her principal trading partners. The largest number of tourists visiting Yugoslavia are European, and several hundred thousand Yugoslav nationals work in these countries. Yugoslavia's credits come mainly from members of the European Community, which has concentrated industrial cooperation and joint ventures in this region, and these constitute a considerable part of Yugoslavia's technology. Even though she has been a nonaligned country for several decades, Yugoslavia has long maintained close relations with all the large integrated groups in Europe.

In addition to associating on a regular basis with the European Free Trade Association (EFTA), Yugoslavia is the only country to have specific treaty relations with both the European Community and the Council for Mutual Economic Assistance (CMEA). It is the only country with a special status in the OECD, participating in the numerous activities of this economic organization of Western countries.

Some parts of Yugoslavia are members of the Alpe-Adria work community, which rallies many regions of Western, Eastern, and neutral countries. A pentagonal association has recently been established to promote cooperation between the five countries of Central and Southeast Europe.

Yugoslavia, as a uniquely European country, and not by geography alone, must take measures to establish further links with Europe in order to become an integral part of future European markets and institutions.

THE ECONOMICS OF EUROPE'S FUTURE

Yugoslavia is aware of her potential position in Europe, and what the future single European market has to offer. This will be an enormous and largely homogenized market of broad and growing economic power. It will be the largest market entity in the world, with almost 350 million inhabitants with great purchasing power. With the disappearance of the last barriers, it should act as a single unit regardless of its multistate composition.

This offers extraordinary potential for a further division of labor, for a high degree of specialization, for utilization of economies of scale in mass production, and for a reduction in costs and more competitive prices. Furthermore, this offers a chance for further business and technological integration. One of the decisive advantages of such an economic community is the potential to intensify scientific research and partially concentrate resources and guidance focused on research. It will also be possible to allocate critical funding for research, which in today's world is one of the conditions for successful operation. In this way, the countries of today's European Community have also readied themselves for participation in world trade. The feedback has yielded a relatively high long-term growth rate for the community.

In this powerful internal market, the European Community has the added advantage of great export and trading potential. Another positive feature, especially for the underdeveloped countries in this integrated group, is the general business reputation enjoyed by the EC among third-world countries. Since most of the EC members have highly efficient economies, it is usually presumed that goods coming from them are of high quality, and if some countries really achieve this, their commercial references are enhanced all over the world. The undeveloped and less developed EC countries have more protection and less exposure to risks than undeveloped and less developed countries outside the EC, for it is not easy to impose trade and other sanctions/restrictions on them.

That products from every member-country are exported to so many countries without tariffs and other barriers is, of course, one of the basic advantages, along with almost free circulation of capital, labor, and technology. However, Europe still does have serious problems. The old continent is in constant danger of technological lag, finding it difficult to follow the multitude of rapid technological advancements taking place in the United States and Japan. Another reason Western Europe lags behind is its larger expenditure on social welfare. In the 1980s, at a ministerial conference of EC and OECD countries, serious studies were done on the impact of a further rise in the proportion of government expenditure on gross national product. Attention was drawn to the danger threatening Europe under its pursuit of social welfare policy, which had initial economic and political advantages but has not been without burdens to the competitive struggle for markets.

Huge government expenditures, especially subsidies for agriculture, and large-scale unemployment threaten Europe, making her more vulnerable to external economic shocks. Therefore there are many advocates of pure market principles, where everything has its real price and everyone is compelled to conduct business as efficiently as possible. Europe has difficulty maintaining and strengthening her competitiveness, especially in the conspicuous economic struggle in the Pacific area.

Although the EUREKA project, a twenty-member West European network formed in 1985 to funnel research and advanced technology between firms and research institutions, has resolutely fought for its economic equality, with partial success, energy consumption after the oil crisis was reduced more per product unit than it was reduced by the direct competitors, the United States and Japan. Despite the more rapid growth in productivity in Yugoslavia than in the United States, no one in the European countries nor even in the European Community feels secure about the future. However, European countries acting together can overcome their difficulties much more easily.

REMOVAL OF OBSTACLES TO BROADER EUROPEAN INTEGRATION

Yugoslavia is determined to be included in an integrated Europe, although there are existing problems. Despite Yugoslavia's presence in Europe and her intense interrelationships and links with the rest of Europe, obstacles to broader integration still exist, both internal and external. These are gradually being removed by Yugoslavia and others.

The Greater Openness of the European Community

Europe is gradually becoming more open. The European Community, which was closed earlier except to fellow members, is obviously expanding its cooperation to include the rest of Europe and the world. The EC is very interested in this development, being aware that although it is becoming one of the largest producers and world markets, it cannot prosper without intensive cooperation with other parts of the world economy.

The EC cooperates with a group of sixty-five African, Caribbean, and Pacific countries, which form a worldwide linkage to a large number of developing countries. It also has cooperative agreements with some Latin American integrated groups. In addition, the EC is pursuing a specific Mediterranean policy, to create a zone of special relations for the development of mutual interests.

Even before the present period, significant links had been established between the European Community and the CMEA. Over a five-year period, the EC imports from CMEA countries alone increased 2.5 times. Now there are fewer theoretical obstacles and a more favorable political climate, with a rapidly increasing volume of mutual trade.

The most significant move the European Community can make is the creation of a single future European economic association for the 1990s. Within this context, further rapprochement between the European Community and EFTA is vitally important.

Those countries that advocated free European trade from in the beginning but, because of their neutral status or political convictions, did not join the bloc-based EEC, formed their own trading group, EFTA. Great Britain initiated this group in an attempt to extricate itself from isolation, being unable to accept the existing conditions for joining the EEC. The EFTA member-countries abolished tariffs on industrial goods in international trade, and after Britain's entry into the EEC, virtually all EFTA countries signed agreements on free trade with the EEC. Today the EC and EFTA countries constitute a broader and more widely integrated Europe.

Neither the EFTA nor the EC is satisfied with the status quo. Both organizations emphasize the character of the Rome treaty (1957) and the words "Europe" and "European nations," implying that the EC perceived itself as relevant to Europe as a whole, not just to EC members. The treaties set forth specific objectives in international relations and extended the geographic area of this integrated grouping to the rest of Europe.

In addition, EFTA had already welcomed the successful inclusion of some of its former members into the EC and expressed satisfaction with the intended creation of a single European market by 1992.

In view of this, the EC stand is that several concentric circles are evolving in Europe and that the EC round off the process. Present in the first circle are twelve EC member countries; in the second, the EFTA countries; in the third, the Mediterranean coutries; and in the fourth, the East European countries, with the process not yet completed.

As a result, the configuration of the European Community is necessarily being changed. Although the community's intent has always been to become a political union as well, this process became more intense in the 1970s. Since then it has maintained a presence on the international scene as a single political entity. In the new world constellation, the EC is losing its bloc character somewhat, becoming more open to a wider range of countries with different political profiles.

The president of the Council of the European Community, Jacques Delors, announced that in light of the sweeping and momentous changes in Eastern Europe, the community would be open to some socialist countries, namely Yugoslavia and Hungary.

Consequently, the EC, or the future single European economic area, is becoming more open, making it possible for Yugoslavia to be more actively involved.

Yugoslavia's Position in the Nonaligned Movement

Another aspect is the political attitude of Yugoslavia, which is vitally linked to the nonaligned movement. This was one of Yugoslavia's strategic targets, organically associated with its commitment to peace and world cooperation, without any military/political/economic blocs, for a world of equal opportunity for all. This target is also one of the foundations of Yugoslavia's defense policy and external security. The determination of Yugoslavia and other countries has not only protected her from foreign interference, attacks, and challenges to her independence, but has made her strive for the right of all to freedom and independence, protection from and prevention of attacks on the sovereignty of countries, and for the sole right of countries to regulate their internal affairs.

This political philosophy and strategy have previously been considered incompatible with membership in bloc-divided integrated economic groups and military-political alliances. However, this is now changing. In the new international climate, the characteristics of the internationally integrated economic groups and institutions are undergoing changes. Also, there is more opportunity for Yugoslavia to participate in these groups and institutions.

Belonging to the nonaligned movement and to a group of developing countries is no longer necessarily incompatible with institutional links to integrated economic groupings. At the time of confrontation with a bipolar world, the basic preoccupation of non aligned countries was to avoid alignment in order to remain free and independent; however, their basic preoccupation today is to leap into this multipolar world. To remain outside the main flow of economic, scientific, and technological development could jeopardize their freedom and independence. No matter how essential, indispensable, or unavoidable, the self-reliance policy holds, and unless it becomes empty rhetoric, the illusion, nonaligned countries cannot move strictly within their own circles. They must whenever possible, communicate on an even wider basis with developed and other countries--a reality of the present-day multipolar world. Nonaligned countries also cannot solve any of their problems alone, nor should they strive to impose their own solutions on the rest of the world under the guise of world peace, disarmament, changes in the world economy, or international economic relations.

For these reasons, Yugoslavia's future entry into an integrated European arena will be an indirect but substantial contribution to the cause of the non aligned countries. Yugoslav foreign policy is appreciated in the world, especially within the non aligned movement, because her further linkage with Europe will contribute to a more universal Europe-- one more open in principle, without exclusions and conditions. This will facilitate the adjustment of other nonaligned countries to a more open future and a more cooperative world.

A weak and economically underdeveloped Yugoslavia would not be able to retain its full independence for long, because in dealing with economically weak countries, the larger and more developed countries find it much easier to adopt policies that bring the weak countries' independence into question. Yugoslavia, too, can no longer be assured a rapid economic development and a competitive position if she remains outside the powerful integration now taking place in Europe. Since an unstable and dependent Yugoslavia is also a threat to the non-aligned movement, her international role makes it imperative to these countries that she be economically and politically strong. If Yugoslavia is able to guarantee this through closer cooperation with Europe, then this cooperation is also in line with her broader political interests. It follows that if Yugoslavia is no longer faced with the dilemma of Europe versus nonalignment, the only possibility is a parallel, synchronized direction.

Yugoslavia is experiencing rapid changes, and earlier obstacles to a more intense integration in Europe have been removed. The European Community's doctrine covers a homogeneous grouping of countries, all of which have multiparty democratic political systems, guaranteed human rights, and economic systems of free initiatives and market forces.

The following explain the direction and motivation for the changes in Yugoslavia:

1. Pressure is mounting to build a multiparty parliamentary political system. Multiparty elections have already been held in some federal units of the country (Croatia and Slovenia), where new authorities have been

established by these elections.   Multiparty elections in other federal republics and in the rest of the country are on the horizon.

2. The remnants of statist economic mechanisms are being abandoned, with a move toward a more free and competitive market.

3. Changes are underway in property relations. Instead of the predominating social ownership or variant of state ownership, there is a transition to private and shareholder ownerhip.

4. Constitutional and statutory frameworks for the protection of human rights and freedoms are being introduced.

5. Efforts are being made to introduce and apply economic mechanisms that have future applications to the single European market; this should make it possible for Yugoslavia and her system to adapt to the European integration trend.

6. Among the most important changes are the almost complete openness to the rest of the world of the Yugoslav economy, the convertibility of the domestic currency, an all-time record level of foreign exchange reserves, and the curbing of inflation to almost zero.

These measures should not only facilitate but accelerate Yugoslavia's entrance into the economic arena of Europe.

JOINING THE EUROPEAN INTEGRATION PROCESS

Despite changes in Europe, especially in Yugoslavia, the question is still open as to how this country will be included in an integrated European community of the future.

It should be noted that these processes and changes are evolving with difficulty.   The West criticizes violations of human rights, especially in Kosovo, which is an autonomous province predominantly inhabited by Albanians.   Furthermore, there are still uncertainties about how to transform social ownership into the kinds of ownership that are more suitable to market economies and free entrepreneurship.

Moreover, sharp inter-nationality clashes continue, hindering the implementation of economic reforms and raising questions its internal political stability. Overcoming these and other problems will not be easy.

Because of these issues, the European Community has not approved Yugoslavia's admission to it, although it does recognize and support the reform process being systematically carried out by the federal government and authorities in some parts of the country. Because of these positive processes, the EC is ready to extend and broaden its contractual links with Yugoslavia, which have functioned since the early 1980s to guarantee close and fairly extensive cooperation.

Reforms in Yugoslavia are supported and financially assisted by large international financial institutions such as the World Bank and the International Monetary Fund.

Yugoslavia is conducting negotiations with the Council of Europe on its future inclusion, although the council now has some reservations because of the human rights violations in Kosovo. However, there is the expectation that Yugoslavia will be admitted to this significant European forum in 1991.

EFTA has recently expressed readiness to open negotiations for the inclusion of Yugoslavia into this European group. This has far-reaching implications for Yugoslavia's future presence in Europe. EFTA constitutes a significant framework for international trade among European countries, and Yugoslavia stands to derive specific benefits from this free trade association. Membership in EFTA, with its rules, internal and external relations, and institutions, would be a historic step--a decisive move forward into a world where the basic motives for existence and economic activity are no longer a fight against the constant threat of poverty but a struggle for a better and richer life. Yugoslavia would take an equal place among the most developed countries.

As an EFTA member, Yugoslavia--long accustomed to living in a close-knit international community and being preoccupied with overcoming her crisis--might expect strong and more direct international support in overcoming her crisis.

Needless to say, the most important component at this juncture is Yugoslavia's openness to one zone of free trade. In spite of the problems necessarily imposed by such changes, these would have a positive effect, acting as an external economic catalyst to compel Yugoslav enterprises and companies to fight to achieve full international competitiveness. At first, this would be a difficult task, but it is the only solution and prospect for the future.

Importantly enough, most EFTA members are neutral countries; this did not occur by chance. Therefore, Yugoslavia's closer links with this grouping would have distinct advantages, along with the possible entry of the EFTA member-countries into the single European economic arena--an integrated European network for the future.

14

Foreign Policy and Changing Times
Radovan Vukadinovic

It is not easy today to write about Yugoslavia's foreign policy, her international position, or the relationship between her reforms and the changes on the international foreign political stage. Yugoslavia is undergoing dramatic political, economic, ideological, and ethnic crises; the country's very survival is at stake. Its foreign policy can scarcely be discussed without immediately raising the question of the veracity of the subject. In these days of general instability and uncertainty, it is much easier to discuss the past than the present, and it is impossible to predict what will happen in the future. Furthermore, the changes taking place in different areas of Yugoslavia raise new questions and problems each day, which may easily refute any previously adopted thesis.

TITO'S FOREIGN POLICY

After World War II, Yugoslavia's foreign policy was closely linked to policy at home. Having emerged from the war with a victor's political power and led by Tito, the country went through several developmental stages, with its domestic and foreign policy closely linked and aimed at resolving certain vitally important issues.

From liberation to the implementation of the Cominform resolution in 1948, Yugoslavia's foreign policy was adjusted to the new regime's demands for the country's reconstruction. Strengthening friendships and cooperation with the Soviet Union and other countries with peoples' democracies forged a closely knit alliance structure. By its very ideological, political, and even panslavonic orientation, Yugoslavia's foreign policy served that group of countries, blazing new trails in Europe to build a new society based on the Soviet, Bolshevik model.

The year was 1948, and the blockade of Yugoslavia by the Cominform countries marked the turning point in Yugoslavia's foreign policy. Despite pressure and open threats from Eastern Europe, its task became twofold: to strengthen ties with the West and to create a new basis for security.

For the survival of the regime and maintenance of the existing authority, both internal and foreign policymakers were preoccupied with acomplishing this, using everything at their disposal. The internal reforms were gradual, progressing only after Yugoslavia had stabilized her international position and obtained some guarantees that the security of Yugoslavia would be one of the political interests of the Western Bloc. Because of the nature of the regime and the climate within the country, internal reform progressed slowly, while foreign policy sought out new allies in the West and strived to strengthen Yugoslavia's position in the United Nations and other international bodies.

Unfortunately, the internal reforms and dynamic foreign policy could not forge ahead of those of other countries at a similar development level. Yugoslavia, preoccupied with survival, moved slowly into a new pattern of relationships. The death of Stalin, in 1953, eliminated this dangerous external threat.

Continuing its first contacts with the newly liberated countries, Yugoslavia's foreign policy, having weathered the battle for survival, concentrated far more energy and dynamism on expanding the range of its international relations to seek new allies and friends. The policy of nonengagement, later to become known as the policy of nonalignment, was conceived as an opportunity to expand Yugoslavia's influence in interntional relations. On the internal stage, self-management was declared the ideology of development, while nonalignment played a corresponding role in international relations. It was believed that the upsurge in the developing countries, based on postwar elan and external accumulation, would inevitably expand the framework of nonalignment. As a policy of nonalliance with the blocs, it would offer vast development possibilities to the many countries in

Asia, Africa, and Latin America.

In the 1960s, from the decolonization and emergence of new countries, Yugoslavia adopted nonalignment as the leading doctrine of her foreign policy and the foundation for her international activities. Despite the euphoria over new friends and allies, who looked upon Yugoslavia as a developed country with an organized political system, guided by President Tito's authority, there were some attempts to press nonalignment into the service of a Yugoslav economic engagement.

Although it was hard to believe that Yugoslavia, which had developed on external accumulation alone, would be able to enter into major investments with developing and nonaligned countries, she entered into just such a commitment. What the critics of nonalignment most censured were the exaggerated value of the nonaligned alliance and the difference between the price of this policy and its actual impact. However, in those times all of us had to obediently accept an established policy as the only choice.

Believing in the alleged international advantages to be gained, as reflected by the expanding circle of cooperating countries, Yugoslavia assumed the leading role among the nonaligned and a major role in the United Nations, with considerable international prestige. At the same time, her leaders also believed that nonalignment would serve a useful purpose on the internal stage.

As a diverse country opting for nonalignment, Yugoslavia acquired all its constituents, including the less highly developed of its republics. At the same time, this political option resolved the dilemma of whom to side with, whether to opt for the West or for the East. Resorting to the so-called "theory of equidistance" made it possible to pursue a largely independent nonalignment policy based on the framework of nonalignment and to freely appraise various international events and the vehicles for international development.

On the international stage, the attitude of nonalignment towards the blocks was notably important. Yugoslavia was able to forge new links in regions where, without nonalignment, she would have found it hard to penetrate. For the Western world, her policy of nonalignment was not always acceptable; it was often a vague concept and frequently dubbed "pro-soviet." Never the less, it was preferable to actual alliance with the Eastern Bloc. Yugoslavia's option to respect the principles of nonalignment and her disassociation from the Eastern bloc was appreciated in the West. This made it possible for Yugoslavia to maintain good relations with both sides, East and West. Even the Eastern Bloc, always hoping Yugoslavia would one day return to the fold, tolerated nonalignment in the belief that its anti-imperalist bias might be used in cooperation against the West under certain circumstances.

In a combination of her internal and international functions, nonalignment long determined the main focus of strategic and practical political considerations in Yugoslav foreign policy. It would last as long as its founding regime. Apart from the respect given by both East and West to Yugoslavia as a nonaligned country, which in some way resolved all possible dilemmas about Yugoslavia's road to development, the relations that developed among the nonaligned countries gave rise to a faint hope of more useful and firmer links among them in the future.

IMPACT OF THE INTERNAL CRISIS ON FOREIGN POLICY

The alarming events following Tito's death in 1980 highlighted the problems a post-Tito Yugoslavia had to contend with. While the relatively monolithic League of communists exited from the ideological stage, a political process began unfolding, with new values and demands for a new internal order. On the economic stage and in national relations, the exploding crisis clearly revealed the mistakes of the past and confirmed the possibility that Yugoslavia's territories might become a battleground similar to the Balkans or Lebanon, as it is in fact today.

These events had a direct impact on Yugoslavia's foreign policy and international position. During the first few years after Tito's death, Yugoslavia's foreign policy was spared open criticism, but it was obvious that the concept of ideologized foreign policy had become untenable. There was some support for disposing of the old foreign policy and creating a new one, although changes on the domestic stage inevitably infringed upon foreign policy as well.

Attacks on Yugoslav foreign policy were mitigated by the authority of President Tito, its main architect, but could not be prevented completely. The new realities in internal relations, and the demands for changes in the economic and political structure, creation of conditions conducive to a free market economy, and a new pluralist political system--all together made an impact on foreign policy. The sheer complexity of the internal factors taken up in various quarters and at various times soon resulted in a deterioration of Yugoslavia's international stature, and her foreign policy activities were weakened by her sociopolitical problems.

The initial differences among Yugoslavia's republics made it clear that foreign/political priorities would soon appear on the agenda. It was a short leap from demands for a reevaluation of Yugoslavia's role to an assault on the government's doctrine and structure. There were those who demanded policy changes and those who opposed change in favor of continuing with the old political and social development principles.

The advocates of change looked upon demands for a new open policy toward Europe as an opportunity to reach modern goals and to break down the old dogmatic ideological system. In this respect, the new foreign policy supported the introduction of a multiparty system and establishment of a free market.

The demands were most often heard from Slovenia and Croatia, to be seconded by the new Yugoslav Premier Ante Markovic, who was in favor of political and economic reform and rapprochement with Europe, pending complete entry.

The disintegration of the League of Communists of Yugoslavia made it possible for this approach to be accepted more quickly. The league had lost its one-time monolithic role in inter-republican quarrels, and as an ideological leader, it had lost its power to act. The creation of new political organs in Slovenia and Croatia, which won in the free elections, paved the way for broad reforms, including reforms in foreign policy.

Advocates of the conservative approach to political change demanded only minor reparatory interventions and claimed that foreign policy needed no changes. They averred that Yugoslav foreign policy had passed the test of time, that all of the global predictions of the nonaligned nations had become reality, and that the end of the Cold War could be considered a victory for nonaligned countries and their policies. Therefore, they argued, there should be no revisions but only some modernizations of foreign policy, since it had, in essence, been a correct one. Tito's sympathizers resisted joining the EEC and criticized regional actions intended to bring some of the republics closer to Western Europe, for example, the work of the Alpe-Adria community and the membership in it of Slovenia and Croatia.

Along with the possibility of Yugoslavia's

rapprochement with Western Europe and participation in general European activity, there were other issues illustrating the collision course between old and new ideals:

1. Debates over establishing diplomatic relations with South Korea, which continued so long that several East European countries established relations ahead of Yugoslavia;

2. Efforts to resume relations with Israel, which also lagged behind those of the East European countries; and

3. Renewal of relations with the Republic of South Africa, which moved at a slow and difficult pace, as well.

In this clash between the old and the new, there are now more opportunities to freely express views, and for the first time since World War II, intellectuals can play a major role in foreign policy discussions. Instead of paeans to nonalignment as the best policy for Yugoslavia, there have now been pleas for changes to foreign policy in almost all milieus. Rapprochement with Europe has won an almost complete intellectual consensus. Realizing that the world and Europe were changing and that Yugoslavia was being left on the sidelines (although it seemed for a while that Yugoslavia was definitely among those bitterly resisting any reforms--in the company of Albania and Romania), the intelligencia determined that the time had arrived to encourage internal changes through foreign policy changes and to strive for the formation of a new society.

There was general criticism of Yugoslavia's main line in foreign policy, and denunciation of it in Croatia and Slovenia, where it was claimed that the line encouraged incompetence and was based mainly on ideology, not professional selection. However, this demand for change, which will be "priority one" in future Croatian and Slovenian policy, is only part of the attempt of these republics to specify views.

Heralding a confederate model of the country's future order, Slovenia and Croatia, without being quite specific, have announced that they have put special policies in regard to general Yugoslav policy in place to be implemented. If there is a switch from a federal (once unified) policy to a confederate state, in which each republic would enjoy statehood on the international stage as well, it becomes clear that this tendency will inevitably impact the very architecture of foreign policy.

It has been stated that the new foreign policy in Slovenia and Croatia stands for the people's interests in these republics. This policy demands entry into Europe, greater regard for the respective minorities of other countries, and equitable interaction with other states and international organizations. It defines the principal boundaries for the new confederate model, which is considered valid for all of Yugoslavia, with its constituents or new states next year.

The desire to break with the old practice, to enable the republics to participate directly in shaping foreign policy and the creation of a confederacy and to enable Croatia and Slovenia to have an independent foreign policy is an important motivator for the exploration of new roads in foreign political action. This desire is part of the internal reforms of these two republics and among the core components of their declarations of new statehood.

INTERNATIONAL CHALLENGES

Apart from these internal currents, one should not forget the new configuration of international affairs and the new definition of Yugoslavia's international position. The changes in relations between the superpowers and their blocs have created a new view of overall international relations. There is probably not a single country unaffected by these changes, which have definitely put an end to the Cold War and its bloc divisions, and resolved some bitter antagonisms. Does this signal the beginning of a new order, in which the states are free to have their own interests--no longer enslaved to predetermined rigid views? This is a matter for debate. Yugoslavia will have to find different policies and abandon her practice of steering a middle course between East and West.

Like many other countries, Yugoslavia will no longer be able to take advantage of her so-called extra-bloc status, because future bloc expansion is not expected in the East or West. What is more, the Eastern Bloc is on its way to extinction, like the dinosaur, although NATO is exploring ways to resuscitate it.

The extensive abandonment of ideology and the demilitarization of international relations change the position of small and middle-sized countries, which now have less opportunity to plan "great" policies. Instead, they must dwell on the preservation of their own national interests. "Sitting on the fence" between East and West is now a thing of the past. Strategically and politically viewed, the East is no more, and Gorbachev's Soviet Union is fighting for survival and in need of financial aid from the West.

Steering a middle course between East and West is no longer feasible. Like many other nonaligned countries, Yugoslavia will have to find the best way to promote her own interests on the international stage. Nonalignment, which for almost thirty years was the guideline for Yugoslav foreign policy, is now a more dubious policy. Many nonaligned countries are in the throes of formidable crises, and the new East-West relations have prevented them from improving their one-time positions. Moral, political, military, and economic help from the East has dried up, and what is more, the formerly socialist countries are now competing avidly with each other for Western aid.

This new trend in East-West relations has also removed any possibility of stalling, while present and future conflicts among the nonaligned no longer involve East-West ideologies. Inevitably, the nonaligned countries will be relegated to the sidelines of world events--abandoned by their former protectors and powerful allies.

The critical economic position of the nonaligned and the impossibility of promoting their mutual cooperation (South-South) has dealt a serious blow to Yugoslavia. She now has neither the opportunity nor the will to develop any line of solidarity, being fully occupied with her own overwhelming problems.

Political cooperation lost importance during the Cold War, and economic cooperation never did produce the expected results. Developments in the world have clearly shown that the centers of new action are only in Europe, Japan, and the United States. With the eyes of the world turned toward Europe in anticipation of new links, nonalignment has fewer and fewer prospects of being accepted as the main line in foreign policy.

Added to this should be the criticism from Slovenia and Croatia and other domestic quarters that nonaligned was always an ideologically tinged policy, having little regard for the interests of the country while steering Yugoslavia toward Africa, not Europe.

Therefore, it is small wonder that the winning

political parties in Slovenia and Croatia have made Europe the main objective of their less than elaborate foreign policy plans, ignoring nonalignment. Now Yugoslavia, the "chairman" of the nonaligned movement, has the least chance of winning support at home for this political option, or for launching any major drives in this direction.

The tide of broad and far-reaching changes, wiping out the socialist order in these countries, also reached Yugoslavia, a country that, together with the Soviet Union and Albania, had had her own autonomous socialist transformation; her own revolution; and since world War II, her own independent character. This very independence has caused her more difficulty in extricating herself from socialism than has been experienced by those countries introduced to the Soviet model via Soviet tanks.

In 1948 Yugoslavia firmly rejected the Soviet Union's policy of dictate and subjugate, and she initiated a series of political and economic reforms unique among the socialist countries. At the same time, she opened her frontiers--striving for a life of greater freedom. This, however, was not enough to allow a normal transformation of the existing socialism into some higher form. Although it would seem that the historical process of abolishing state socialism has involved Yugoslavia, despite the various ways some of her constituents are ending their own brand of socialism, the road leading to a free market and a multiparty system is the only viable alternative for Yugoslavia's future.

Although Yugoslavia followed a different path--socialist as opposed to Bolshevik, her self-management, nonalignment, and total people's defense were avenues for rejection of the existing Soviet model, rather than efforts to build something completely different and more suited to the Yugoslav experience.

EUROPE AS A SOLUTION

The term Europe is now in vogue in Yugoslavia and has become widely used, with its distinctive political, economic, cultural, and social connotations. There is virtually no political party or movement not operating without the term Europe or European. This emphasizes that Yugoslavia's only chance to extricate herself from her present difficulties is for the country, or some of it, to reach out to Europe.

Europe has become a synonym for modern and successful development. However, rapprochement with Europe must be a gradual, bilateral, and rational process. The desire to enter Europe as soon as possible, most often meaning the European Economic Community, has subordinated all other plans in the cry for "Europe now."

For years Yugoslavia has pursued a different, virtually global foreign policy, geared to distant regions and different civilizations. Now, in the middle of her crisis, she has turned to Europe for a way out that can only be European and in Europe.

Motivated by turbulent events in the very heart of Europe, by the changes in overall international relations, and by the seriousness of her own domestic crises, Yugoslavia has more recently sent very clear signals through her diplomats and leading statesmen that she is willing to approach the European Economic Community. In support of this, a memorandum was submitted requesting that Yugoslavia be granted the status of an associate member of the EEC. However all of this comes at a time when numerous foreign and internal political problems in the EEC offer no immediate prospects for changing institutional cooperation with Yugoslavia.

The EEC is preoccupied with tendering more substantial aid to Hungary and Poland, where it is following with attentive concern the relations in the new Germany and the aspirations of Czechoslovakia for membership, with Bulgaria and Romania not far behind. There are also problems in relations within the EEC itself, because of the issue of a new Germany and the announcement that Great Britain may renounce some forms of integration, though continuing to support the idea of one Europe, with reservations about accepting it economically.

Given the present degree of political crisis, and lack of the political and economic elements that are a minimum requirement for possible association, Yugoslavia has no hope of joining the EEC in the immediate future, in spite of all of the demands and its by-word of "Europe now." While the whole country is torn by division and strife, burdened by economic crisis and by the unsettled conditions in Kosovo, Yugoslavia can certainly not yet expect full membership. If the same political, social, ideological, and economic climate prevails in 1992, her prospects will be equally grim for acceptance.

In the Yugoslavia of today, a cold war is taking place among its constituents, with all of the signs of a genuine cold war in ideology, politics, and economics. The climate of the Balkans is one of neither war nor peace, and the proponents of the various political ideologies are each pulling national strings. There is also the unsettled agenda the EEC has made a condition for possible membership: a multiparty system, human rights and freedoms, and complete acceptance of a free market and all its mechanisms. The EEC stands firm on all of these issues. If Kosovo is added to the list, one can easily understand the circumspection prevailing, and the diplomatic support to Yugoslav efforts cannot conceal all of the unresolved problems, which prevent Yugoslavia from establishing a closer institutional association.

It could be said that the path to rapprochement with Europe should be sought at home, but only if Yugoslavia uses these premises to solve her own internal economic, political, and social problems. Then she might be considered a serious future candidate for formal association with the European Community. This is even more pertinent today, because the community has to consider not only its role in 1992, but the overall trends in East Europe.

In the drive to link up with the EEC, only those countries capable of instant economic and political adjustments and reshuffling can anticipate more favored treatment. Although Yugoslavia long ago initiated many of the reforms now taking place in Eastern Europe, she has no edge in the keen competition to gain the favor of the rich West. The European Community will insist on close scrutiny of candidates for admission as new members, especially their social and political development toward a Western-style democracy and a free market. This is the price exacted for establishing more favorable relations with the EEC.

With all of the dynamic trends at play in Europe and in Yugoslavia's own internal development, there will have to be a successful combination of foreign political activities with a free internal democratic openness. If Yugoslavia achieves a multiparty structure with full respect for human rights and freedoms, and if she manages to create a free market, it is irrelevant whether she has been granted associate member status now or later.

The most important thing is to show an honest intent to make changes in the country and to strive for political and economic actions based on West European patterns. The European Community cannot remain aloof or let countries on the fringes of

European development be left to go their separate ways. It is imperative that the new Europe of today steadily integrate and bridge the gap between East and West, not only to ensure the successful emergence of Europe as one great "common house" but also to broaden and reach out for the Europe that until now has developed successfully within the boundaries of the Twelve.

Yugoslavia should carefully monitor all European processes and share in all forms of regional association in order to seek functional contracts with all parts of Europe. This should not only facilitate the implementation of new standards at home, but it should help in staying abreast of general European standards. She can then utilize the political goodwill still evident among most of the EEC members and achieve much more than by rash demands for immediate membership, which could provoke negative reactions.

Clearly the EEC will not be able to close its doors to all nonmembers; the current processes in Europe will inevitably affect its the new configuration. Here is Yugoslavia's chance to wisely appraise development trends and to use every concrete opportunity to establish relations, linking herself more closely to processes in the EEC countries. This will be a long road, but one offering opportunities for success both in the European Community and with Yugoslavia's own unsettled domestic problems.

Can Brussels seriously consider partial Yugoslav demands for entry or demands for only some parts of the country to join the community? Politically the community still recognizes a complete Yugoslavia, wanting to see Yugoslav integrity preserved and visualizing association with only one country. Economic factors will not be favorable for allowing parts of Yugoslavia to enjoy privileges in a limited association. Unfortunately, even the developed parts of Yugoslavia have no comparative advantages that might alter political appraisals and compel Brussels to agree to the separate inclusion of one or two parts. So far, there have been no partial memberships in the EEC, even where the EEC has supported a regional policy of association on a multinational scale (the Alpine Community, Alpe-Adria). The community has always sought the expansion of its participants and new elements.

Undoubtedly, the European Community is interested in Yugoslavia, which will impact on the search for the most positive links or networks, either through expanded cooperation or through full membership at some unspecified future time. The European Community demonstrated this interest as far back as 1968, when, fearing further Soviet incursions after the invasion of Czechoslovakia, it concluded an agreement with Yugoslavia to tender economic and financial aid on her behalf. Of course, times have changed, and Yugoslavia is no longer the vehicle for the most liberal and dynamic currents among the socialist countries of Europe, and neither is there any danger, real or imagined, of Soviet aggression.

Intervention in Yugoslavia, once the alleged fondest wish of the Soviet leadership, has been obviated by new trends in relations in Europe, new Soviet policy, and the preoccupation of Soviet leaders with domestic problems.

Today there is a different danger on the horizon, which has been created by internal events in Yugoslavia. The European Community is gravely concerned over Yugoslavia's domestic situation, which, if it were to deteriorate, could have an immediate and profound effect on some EEC members. The move to make visas for entry into West Germany compulsory, already a policy in France, is a reflection of efforts to keep the possible wave of unrest away from Western Europe's doorstep. The question is whether this is possible. Besides its adverse effect on higher forms of cooperation, the threat of internal instability will also force planners in Brussels to think seriously about relations with Yugoslavia.

The European Community can no longer be an oasis of peace and prosperity, isolated from general European trends. For that matter, the European federalists always wanted to see a united Europe, and now is their chance to demonstrate in reality how they imagined this would be.

Radical changes in some of the East European countries, and even in the Soviet Union, have raised the question of what is to be done about these countries. What will their future status be? Is it possible for Hungary and Poland to be simultaneously active in some areas of cooperation within the EEC and still be members of Comecon and the Warsaw Pact? The ultimate solution would be for new processes to emerge, to cause all of the countries to rally around the European Community. Should this remote possibility become a reality, it would be a chance for Yugoslavia to join this group with all of the other countries of Europe.

Until this happens and the EEC has decided what its future development strategy will be, it would be best for Yugoslavia to concentrate on cooperating with the neutral countries of Europe. It is a good thing that there is no European country that does not belong to the economic integration groupings. The neutral countries of Europe are rallied within EFTA, intent on improving mutual cooperation despite the dangers this free trade mechanism is exposed to daily. These countries have managed to conclude an agreement in their traditional links with the EEC. Regardless of the new stages of cooperation within the community, it is certain that if EFTA survives, it will enjoy preferential treatment. So far, the European Community has shown that it is interested in cooperation with the EFTA and that the countries that are party to these agreements enjoy many advantages.

EFTA membership is easier to achieve than membership in the European Community. If Yugoslavia joins, she will create a sound basis for (1) development of new economic relations, (2) maintenance of her political positions, (3) a visible profile in Europe, and (4) membership in a larger community, along with Turkey and Albania, and its future. As a result, the opportunity to join the EEC would be enhanced, and it would help open the doors to complete European integration, if this indeed ever does occur. These countries that are party to these agreements enjoy many advantages.

By creating a united market, the European Economic Community will enter a new developmental stage, with more economic and political power, and possibly establish its own common defense in an isolated and closed process, confined to the boundaries of the European community.

As a European country in these turbulent times, when new foundations are being built for East-West relations, Yugoslavia is threatened by conflicts. The crisis cannot be weathered by just striving to join the EEC, which has its own problems, both internal problems those created by the new international configurations. The EEC can certainly be helpful to Yugoslavia in dealing with growing pains in her attempt to modernize. However, even if Yugoslavia were the only East European country seeking assistance, the EEC would find it difficult to meet all of the demands.

The lines of the hopeful waiting for the gates of Brussels to open have become longer. Although there are differences among the various applicants, all of them obviously look upon the EEC as a vehicle to more rapid extrication from their problems and a firmer handhold on modern development.

Despite all of her strife and internal divisiveness, Yugoslavia does have better prospects of an economic and political character, but the national question has blocked many of these advantages and definitely obfuscated all that was once associated with Yugoslavia's international reputation.

Today Yugoslavia has to share the benevolence of Western Europe with the other East European countries, the "new democracies," which have begun their quest for membership in the EEC. This means that Yugoslavia will have to fight for her new place, largely by making the appropriate moves in internal policy.

The popular by-words of "now" or "today," for demanding entry into Europe have produced no notable results. The EEC has its own criteria: it is cautious in the admission of any new member, and certainly wants to avoid involvement in any crisis.

The best and quickest way for Yugoslavia to get closer to the EEC is to deal unsuccessfully with the situation at home. Had Yugoslavia applied for membership in the EEC during the "golden seventies," the member-nations would have rejoiced. Today, however, there is no wish to discuss even institutional rapprochement.

The climate for a new approach to the EEC will only be created if Yugoslavia's program of extensive political, economic, and social reform is seriously implemented and if citizens throughout the country can live and work normally. Otherwise, the EEC will be even cooler to Yugoslavia's overtures and the new East European democracies will outdistance Yugoslavia, while regardless of all the battle cries of various colors and parties within Yugoslavia, Europe may withdraw even further.

CONCLUSION

Whether there will be a Yugoslav federation attempting to survive on the new democratic foundation of confederalism, or a Yugoslavia that is breaking up, is the question the future holds.

If the confederate model is adopted, foreign policy will certainly be different, not only because of many internal and external factors, but also because of past experiences. In the new era, the national interests of the constituent republics--the states--will be the principal guidelines to which all other demands will be subordinated at home and abroad, to culminate in a pattern for national foreign policy. It will be a long time before a confederal model of foreign policy becomes a reality. There will have to be a lot of compromise, many sacrifices, and great wisdom on the part of its political architects. One can then conclude that the content, priorities, and main thrust of this new policy will have to be subjected to major transformations, with the mechanism that creates and implements it reflecting more wisdom and greater knowledge than it has so far.

New times require new policies, and new policies can only be created by new people with the talents, understanding, and skills to build a confederacy that will represent a contractual relationship among sovereign states. If such a confederacy can be built, a new form of international action may emerge on Yugoslav soil. This model of creating new units and delineating their sovereignty could give new meaning to the term "balkanization," and that this time the word would have an affirmative character. For it should not be forgotten that if there is to be a "Lebanon-ization" of Yugoslavia, associated with her disintegration, it will not happen in any of its variations without a years-long drama, as in the Lebanon of today.

15

European Integration and Yugoslav Reform

Ljubisa S. Adamovic

Economic reform in Yugoslavia, as accepted in 1989, was considered the last in a series of reforms beginning with the break in Cominform in 1948. To many observers and analysts, Yugoslavia seemed to be lagging behind the other ex-socialist countries of Eastern Europe and the Soviet Union in the timing and nature of its reforms. In the late 1980s developments in Yugoslavia were different in many ways from those in other countries of Eastern Europe and in the Soviet Union. Most economic changes, such as the market mechanism, had already been introduced in Yugoslavia in the 1950s and early 1960s. The results had been varied and cyclical, with the Yugoslav economy and society slowly absorbing the many changes in policy designed to rescue its fledgling market economy.

At the same time, the political decentralization and democratization process, while less than perfect when compared with the operational conditions of Western market economies, has had a positive internal and external impact. For example, the development of the private sector in agriculture and the creation of a small business sector in manufacturing and services propelled the country's economy toward more liberal economic cooperation abroad. The advantages of this included freedom of travel, migration, and emigration, and a higher standard of living than in other ex-socialist countries. This made it possible for the country to absorb the shocks caused by the collapse of its so-called Communist regime and consequently, the collapse did not provoke any major internal socioeconomic and political tensions. In this respect, the changes in Yugoslavia can be compared with the "velvet" revolution in Czechoslovakia in 1989.

On the other hand, the disintegration of one-party rule in Yugoslavia has opened up a Pandora's box of ethnic problems for the country, which could have a crucial impact on the success of economic reform.

THE INTEGRATION OF EUROPE OR THE DISINTEGRATION OF YUGOSLAVIA?

The economic integration process in Western Europe has a serious impact on the way the Yugoslav economy operates. After World War II, the three leading economic partners of Yugoslavia were Italy, the USSR, and West Germany, representing the members of the initial group of six. Yugoslavia was the first country from the East to establish contractual relations with the EEC, which it did in 1970. As in other areas and relations with the EEC, Yugoslavia began her process of cooperation much earlier than any of the other formerly socialist countries. Because of current tensions among various ethnic (national) groups in Yugoslavia, better institutional arrangements for dealing with the EEC could be found by other Eastern European Countries than Yugoslavia has found.

However, it is important to differentiate between institutional arrangements and real level of cooperation. An analysis of its actual affairs reveals that in real terms that Yugoslavia is much better integrated with the EEC than any other East European country. The level of integration, as measured in trade, tourism, capital flows, technology imports from EEC countries, and the permanent presence of Yugoslav labor (guest workers) since the early 1960s in EEC countries, leaves little doubt about the integration between the EEC and Yugoslavia. The high level of information flow is based on personal experience and on direct contracts between the millions of citizens of the EEC countries and Yugoslavs. It is possible to claim that the quality of relationships between Yugoslavia and the EEC should be judged not only on an institutional basis and on cooperation--easily quantified--but on types of relationships, which cannot be quantified.

The greatest barrier to improved relations between Yugoslavia and the EEC is the current political climate in Yugoslavia. At a time when other East European countries are striving to improve relations with the EEC, Yugoslavia is in a "lame duck" position, because free elections did not take place in all parts of the country. In the republics of

Slovenia and Croatia, where free elections did occur, disintegration has been pronounced. Pressure has been exerted on the rest of the country: adopt a policy of Confederacy or Slovenia and Croatia will abandon the Yugoslav Federation.

Under these conditions, it is understood that neither the Federal Government of Yugoslavia nor the EEC Commission is able to enter into prolonged debate over the Yugoslav-EEC relationship. In their campaign to secede, representatives from these two republics have sought support from abroad for secession, although it has not been given. On more than one occasion, U. S. and West European leaders have declared to the world that they prefer to see Yugoslavia integrated within its existing borders. They have shown no interest in changing the borders of the various nations within Yugoslavia. At the same time, one assumes that the attitude of outsiders cannot be expected to keep the country integrated if the member states prefer to disassociate themselves.

These winds of unrest in Yugoslavia are not totally new, nor can they be attributed to the absence of a free democratic political system under the socialist regime after World War II. In each ethnic (national) group, pro-Yugoslavia and anti-Yugoslavia attitudes have been present since the nineteenth century. As a matter of fact, since 1918 enormous energy has been expended debating the pros and cons of Yugoslav nations living side by side together. Extreme dissatisfaction, even hate, exploded during World War II, when the Nazi-created Independent State of Croatia organized pogroms and annihilation of Serbs, Jews, and gypsies on an unprecedented scale in European history. Although the killings could be attributed to a minority of Croats (the Ustasi movement), the majority of Croats did not object to the carnage. Whether a rational approach toward the unity of Yugoslavia will prevail is debatable.

Croatia reacted to the disintegration on mainly an emotional and political level, while in Slovenia, the disintegration was nurtured by expectations of economic improvement--a prospect something like leaving one's poor relatives to live by themselves. On many occasions, supporters of Slovenian independence have held the possibility of closer integration within the EEC as a trump card, to win Slovenian popular support for leaving Yugoslavia. However, during the second half of 1989 and through 1990, there was a cooling-off period in Slovenia, which was prompted by the refusal of the EEC to discuss relations with individual regions. A withdrawal from Yugoslavia would cause Slovenia to loose a guaranteed market for its manufacturing industry. Slovenia has 1.7 million people mainly employed in manufacturing/services, with a large market of 24 million people. Loosing that market would mean selling much more in Western Europe, where the competitors are not relatively weak manufacturing producers from Croatia, Serbia, and Bosnia, but strong Western European industry.

As secession from Yugoslavia gained support, representatives of Slovenia had to face up to the problem of future borders with Austria and Italy. These problems, especially with Italy, are to be confronted very soon by secessionists from Croatia. Making no attempt to sugar coat the message, several voices from Italy have made it be known that the London and Rapallo treaties were concluded between Yugoslavia and Italy, not between Italy and separate regions of Yugoslavia.

All things considered, the Slovenian and Croatian movement to secede from Yugoslavia has spread to the Serbs, as evidenced by the attitude that if Slovenes and Croats do not care for Yugoslavia, why should the Serbs care. Before Yugoslavia was formed, the Serbs had two states: the Kingdom of Serbia and the Kingdom of Montenegro. Slovenia never had been a state, and Croatia had lost its statehood in the twelfth century; both were provinces in Austria-Hungary. If secession takes place, internal frontiers among the republics in Yugoslavia will have to be revised.

Despite the general integration process in Europe, especially in Western Europe, it is likely that Yugoslavia in its present structure may cease to exist. Solutions may be found either in a different democratic free market or in a multi-party system state, based on a democratic federal treaty, or a totally different political geography. It is to be hoped that whichever solution is found, the answer will have an interfacing of patience and democratic procedure, for the other alternative could very well be civil war.

During 1990 it was easy to understand why no important agreement has taken place between the EEC and Yugoslavia, and why Yugoslavia seems to be much slower to cooperate with the EEC than several other East European countries.

ECONOMIC REFORM AND CAPITAL IMPORTS

Because of reforms in the mid-1960s, leaving the

dogmatic socialist economic system and introducing a new trend of cooperation abroad, Yugoslavia became a trailblazer. The reform movements met with resistence form special interest groups because of its threat to vested interests. In addition, the introduction of a market economy met with opposition from student movements in 1968 and had to be delayed.

A positive event was the introduction of legislation enabling importation of foreign capital. Regardless of how revolutionary a step it was, however, imports have not been encouraging, either for the Yugoslavs or for foreign owners within the joint business venture framework. This was confirmed from 1968 to 1988, when only 386 joint contracts were finalized, for a total value of about $1 billion U.S. These investments were in credit form, and until 1987, with only $418 million invested in the Yugoslav economy, the balance was paid off.

In an unofficial beginning of the new reforms of 1989, legislation on foreign investments was changed in late 1988 and made compatible with world standards. Interestingly enough, despite the Yugoslav inflation and political instability, once capital imports had been brought into line with the standards that foreign investors were familiar with, they began to climb. For the first fourteen months that these new rules were in place, 555 contracts involving foreign investments were concluded. From January to mid-June 1990, another 1,017 contracts were arranged. Ignited by different legal constraints and lower inflation, this one-and-a-half-year period had generated more imported foreign capital than the previous twenty-one years under the old capital import system. The total value of capital imports under the new legal framework is about $1.5 billion. Thus, the approximate average value of a contract is a relatively low $1 million U. S. One possible reason for the low individual investment by foreign firms is the recession in the Yugoslav economy. Total investment activities in the country are also at a low level, especially since Yugoslavia is still not on firm footing in the world capital market, even though the country does have relatively large foreign exchange reserves and current payments to foreigners. The more efficient banking system and the privatization of the economy should be among the first lessons to be learned from Western Europe by Yugoslav policymakers.

Considering the current stagnation of the Yugoslav economy and the partial price paid for controlling inflation, along with the reduction in production of about 10 percent, an encouraging signal to potential foreign investors is not being sent. The lack of political stability and the unclear political future of the country slow down potential investor programs. In spite of this negative climate, there are a growing number of foreign investors in Yugoslavia. This indicates that (1) Increased competition on the world market is pressing investors not to ignore a side market of 24 million people in southern Europe, and (2) current investment in a troubled economy is to be considered more in the nature of a reservation for a seat than of the purchase of a ticket.

This means that foreign investors consider Yugoslavia to be a strong potential market, and once political tensions are over, more capital imports are to be expected. At the same time, Yugoslavia has lost some of its prime value for foreign investors. For decades it was the only open communist country, but now practically all of Eastern Europe and the Soviet Union is open; consequently, the general rating of Yugoslavia on the world capital market is by definition lower than it was before 1988.

Capital import in Yugoslavia will also depend very much on the privatization process. Instead of being overwhelmed by the idea of having several special trade-free zones in the country to attract foreign investors, Yugoslavia, as a European country, should take a closer future look at the EEC countries. The whole national economy should be open to foreign investments along the "rules of the game" of the EEC. Foreign investors are most comfortable in the countries where they can find a similar social and financial niche. To provide them with special rights in free-trade areas (custom-free zones) would mean that the natives would not have all of the rights that the foreigners would have, which would indeed discourage many potential foreign investors.

Another important concern is privatization, which does not have a serious role in the Yugoslav economy, nor in some of the constituent republics. According to some of the public signals from Croatia and Serbia, the trend is to create a state property sector instead of privatization. There is no doubt that in some areas the state may own enterprises and institutions that deliver goods and services; however, if what once was social property (<u>drustvena svojina</u>) is to become state property (<u>drzavna svojina</u>) before it can be open to privatization, then matters may be going from bad to worse. In this process, the only gem that sparkles in this process for foreign investors is the fact that foreign partners can deal with one big partner from the Yugoslav side. But would the state (government) be considered a preferred partner? Doubtful.

If the privatization process takes place, according to the Law on Social Capital (<u>Zakon</u> <u>o</u> <u>drustvenom</u> <u>kapitalu</u>) and its latest changes, foreign investors could be discouraged from entering into a project whereby they would have to face many small partners on the Yugoslav side, because the shares of certain enterprises would be distributed among their current and former employed workers. The total value of public property to be privatized is about $180 billion U. S. Woods, mineral deposits, and natural resources would not be privatized. According to the government's program, that value could be sold for about 75 billion, but in practical terms, it would bring in about $30 billion, if the employed population accepts 15 percent of its earned income in share form.

The inflow of foreign investments will depend very much on the fiscal policy of Yugoslavia. It is naive to expect foreign investors to adjust to the Yugoslav system of taxation, which includes two components: straight taxation and a system of earmarked contributions (<u>doprinosi</u>) based on the number of persons employed or on the payroll. Needless to say, to a domestic or foreign investor the system of contributions is just a euphemism for double taxation. Contributions to payroll taxation make labor in Yugoslavia very expensive. Add to that a personal income tax based on the progressive taxation principle, which means that every high-quality performance is overtaxed. As a rule, personal income tax is not known until the end of the year, so that individual adjustments are almost impossible. Since it is hard to find a market economy in Europe with triple taxation of labor (payroll contributions, corporate income tax, and personal income tax), one of the most abundant components in the Yugoslav economy, instead of being relatively cheap, becomes very expensive and makes capital comparatively inexpensive.

Yugoslavia has not yet factored into her economy a way to improve cooperation with the EEC countries. As a result of the taxation system, labor is expensive for the employer, while employees are dissatisfied with the low level of wages and salaries. To attract foreign investors and to utilize capital owned by Yugoslavs in foreign banks and at home, it is critical that a fair and stable system of taxation be implemented.

Yugoslavia must avoid double taxation of the foreign investor, and the Yugoslav taxation system must be made compatible with the systems of the EEC and other market economy countries so that foreign investors in Yugoslavia can avoid another taxation in their country of origin.

Foreign investors are concerned about regulations on the labor market in Yugoslavia. That the so-called technological surplus of labor cannot be left unemployed has become a burden for many Yugoslav firms. For the potential foreign investor, this principle may become an unbridgeable barrier.

There are still many unclear variables in banking that make entrance into this arena less attractive to potential investors. A Yugoslav citizen cannot be the founder of a local bank; this does not encourage foreigners to invest in the banking business, despite the nonexistence of legal barriers to do so.

The parameters for real estate investments are still not clearly defined for foreign investors because of certain conditions that have to be met.

From manufacturing to real estate, there is a broad potential for change. Yugoslavia has to become more open to external economic impulses. Once this is done, the capital inflows will help to activate and streamline domestic production and may contribute to faster economic growth. Yugoslavia's past and future relations with the EEC should help drive her economy toward better performance in the future.

YUGOSLAVIA'S COMPARATIVE ADVANTAGE

In an analysis of Yugoslavia's current position and its economy under economic reform, and Yugoslavia's potential to become an integral part of the EEC through Yugoslav and foreign sources, it could be concluded that most analysis take the traditional line of economic reasoning from the classical industrialization process of the 1870s to the 1970s. Most envision Yugoslavia operating within a traditional production framework, ignoring the results of the third technological revolution. However, economic reform in Yugoslavia is unfolding at the beginning of the Information Age, the most valuable asset being its resourceful people--human capital. The training of Yugoslavia's people is excellent. If economic reform liberates her most valuable resource--human knowledge and ideas, she can then join the information age. Heretofore Yugoslavia has been more open and less under bureaucratic control than the other ex-socialist countries, which has produced two mixed economic results:

1. The country in general and people in particular are relatively well exposed to high technology.

2. The freedom of movement and mobility of labor, including temporary or permanent emigration, has caused the exodus of some of the country's brightest minds.

Economic reform will be successful only if it helps to create a climate of individual and entrepreneurial freedom. This is what is needed to motivate the creative people of the nation to translate their dreams and ideas into creative action. The need for capital imports is dictated more by the necessity to import new technology than for capital alone. It would be difficult to claim that Yugoslavia does not have the capital; the roads, communications networks, public utilities, education and health systems, factories, and other forms of embodied capital are already accumulated. As a matter of fact, a large part of the existing capital has not been fully tapped. What is now needed is more freedom, a climate of security, and conditions that will encourage daring people to take risks, to succeed and meet the challenges or to fail. Freedom to pursue entrepreneurial success is now a critical growth factor in Yugoslavia, for without it, economic reform will not be successful, nor can the full resource potential of existing Yugoslav capital and the creative capacity of her people be realized.

The most important real capital in Yugoslavia in 1990 is creative citizens. Yugoslav enterprises and their entrepreneurs should be allowed to fail and face bankruptcy, because the failures are almost as important to economic growth as the successes are. Lessons from failures are far more impressive than lessons from success. New knowledge is being generated. The history of economic growth has shown that only those who learn how to earn profits can learn how to make the best use of those profits.

When the role of natural resources declines, the role of the human mind and imagination expands. The current industrial revolution based on information has expanded the role of mind over matter; what once was a source of comparative advantage in important natural resources has now declined as a share value in modern economies. As a result, the focus of

209

geopolitics, territory (physical and military control), international economic relations, and decline in the value of raw materials have caused these changes. The location of transnational companies and capital has become more flexible; location is not necessarily tied to "where the action is," because the international system of transportation and communications can be controlled from a different place. The same principle is valid for capable people, because if conditions are not favorable, they can move far away and use their talents elsewhere. Technology has forced these changes, which are still beyond the reasoning of reformers in the ex-socialist countries, including Yugoslavia. It has to be understood that this new technology is bringing a different social strata with it. The balance of social power, national and international, is tilting in favor of the entrepreneurs and the creative element in Yugoslav society, at the expense of politicians, bureaucrats, and the military.

WESTERN AID TO YUGOSLAV REFORM

Western nations, especially the members of the EEC, are expected to provide subsidies to the governments in East European countries and the Soviet Union, to facilitate the transition from a centrally planned economy to a market economy, although there has been far more rhetoric than financial assistance.

Yugoslavia's membership in the European Bank, especially created to provide credit lines for ex-socialist countries, has been accepted by the bank foundation. However, the question is, how much Yugoslav policymakers should expect to obtain in aid, from straight grants to soft credit lines?

In the past, foreign aid has sometimes been a double-edged sword. Although the development of the Yugoslav economy since 1948 was different from that of the Soviet Union and Eastern Europe, had such capital inflow been available then, Yugoslavia would probably have been wise not to rush to accept it.

The experience of Yugoslavia and the third-world countries with foreign aid programs reveals both the potential for and the limitations of a noncommercial transfer of funds. As the current economic literature tries to illuminate what industrial development can do, it also tends to question the ruling thesis of the theory of economic development about the vicious circle of poverty. Whatever the theoretical outcome of this analysis might be, Yugoslavia is far ahead of the third-world countries, except those that joined the number of the newly industrialized countries, and also far ahead of East European countries and the Soviet Union, which participate in international economic relations on commercial principles only.

Individuals, groups, local communities, and countries have emerged from misery to prosperity without any donations or aid. Practically all of the developed countries of today were once poor and began their development without subsidies. Many countries have been able to recover from the devastating destruction of war, without receiving any aid from abroad. Economic progress does not depend solely on the amount of funds to be invested. Unfortunately, the current structure of the Yugoslav economy shows many cases of abuse of funds for investment--often borrowed at high interest rates or received as subsidies. For many investment projects, the main criterion has not been economic efficiency alone, but political favors and impact (_politicke_ _fabrike_).

Poor individuals and poor nations are able to generate sufficient savings to improve their well-being if two conditions are met: (1) a strong motivation to improve their living standards and (2) a favorable climate created by government to ensure that the results of their efforts can enjoy legal security. The issue of social property must therefore be resolved to guarantee the success of economic reform in Yugoslavia. Property rights have to be clearly defined and well protected. Even countries with high inflation rates and with high commercial risks are attractive to domestic and foreign investors, as long as the owners' property rights are respected. The rate of capital inflow into many Asian, African, and some socialist countries, with potential political risk but with protected property rights, shows which areas of the Yugoslav economic system need improvements.

Yugoslavia's unstable political climate in the fall of 1990, along with the unclear status of public or social property, have brought about a substantive reduction in investment. Yugoslav authorities must solve the problems of barriers inhibiting the inflow of foreign capital and misuse of domestic capital. Repatriation of Yugoslav owners' capital from abroad and its investment in the Yugoslav economy should be considered.

Capital flight from Yugoslavia deserves special attention. According to estimates by the German

Banking Association, Yugoslav citizens have deposits of close to 90 billion DM on account in Western Europe. The major part of this amount is earned and saved by Yugoslavs employed in Western Europe. The term <u>capital flight</u> is not correct in the literal sense, because the bottom line is that earned funds are not being brought back to Yugoslavia but kept abroad. However, the general economic connotation is one of capital flight, although technically the funds do not leave the country.

On both economic and psychological grounds, Yugoslavia should not rely on subsidies from abroad, because soft loans or open/hidden subsidies, if given to governments, are not distributed to the population as a whole. Instead, the government is given more resources, more power, and more potential for patronage to special interest groups. This causes economic life to become even more political--the last thing the Yugoslav economy and society need. The broader the ethnic and cultural differences and conflicts within a country, the more dangerous it is to politicize its economic life; in this Yugoslavia could serve as a textbook case.

By providing a favorable climate for domestic investors, Yugoslavia can send a positive signal to her potential foreign investors who will then participate in and accelerate the march of economic progress and, as participants, help forge acceptable policies. This will be the most realistic way to integrate the Yugoslav economy and allow it to become a more fundamental part of the European economic process, regardless of future changes to her institutional status in the EEC.

Bibliography

Adamovic, Ljubisa S. "Savremena Administracija."
 [Contemporary administration] In _Integration and Disintegration in the World Economy_ (Belgrade, 1987): 40.

_____. "Intervju." [Interview] no. 240 (Belgrade, 1990).

Bajt, Aleksander. _Samoupravni oblici drustvene svojine_ [Self-management forms of social ownership]. Ljubljana: Globus, 1988.

Baletic, Zvonimir, Bozo Marendic, Nikola Obradovic, Dragomir Vojnic, and Stjepan Zdunic, eds. _Koncepcija i Mehanizmi Strukturnog Prilagodjavanja_ [The concept and mechanisms of structural adjustment]. Zagreb: Economics Institute and the Social Planning Board of Croatia, 1988.

Ballasa, Bela. _Structural Adjustment Policies in Developing Economies_. World Bank Staff Working Paper no. 464. Washington, D.C.: The World Bank, 1981.

_____. "Newly Industrializing Developing Countries after the Oil Crisis." _Weltwirtschaftlick Archiv. Bd._ 117, no. 1 (1981).

Becker, Gary S. _The Economics of Discrimination_. Chicago: University of Chicago Press, 1957.

Borchardt, K. D. _European Unification: the Origins and Growth of the European Community_. Luxembourg: Office for Official Publications of the European Communities, 1987.

Breton, Albert. "The Economics of Nationalism." _Journal of Political Economy_ 72 (1964): 376-86.

Buchanan, James M., and Gordon Tullock. _The Calculus of Consent_. Ann Arbor: University of Michigan Press, 1962.

Colberg, Marshall R. "Property Rights and

Motivation: United States and Yugoslavia."
Proceedings and Reports, Center for Yugoslav-
American Studies, Research, and Exchanges, Florida
State University, vol. 12-13 (1978-1979): 52-58.

Colberg, M. R., and D. R. Forbush. Business
Economics: Principles and Cases. 7th ed.
Homewood, Ill.: Irwin, 1987.

Comisso, E. T. Workers' Control under Plan and
Market. New Haven: Conn.: Yale University Press,
1979.

Commission of the Federal Social Councils for
Economic Stabilization Problems. Fundamental
Elements of the Long-Term Program of Economic
Stabilization. 4 vols. Belgrade: Centar za
Radnicko Samoupravljanje, 1982-83.

"Contemporary Developments in Western Europe: The
Position and Role in International Relations and
Interests in Yugoslavia." Report, Center for
Strategic Studies, Belgrade, 1986.

Dennis, Mueller C. Public Choice II. Cambridge:
Cambridge University Press, 1989.

Dimitrijevic, Dimitrije, and George Macesich. Money
and Finance in Contemporary Yugoslavia. Foreword
by Milton Friedman. New York: Praeger, 1973.

____. Money and Finance in Yugoslavia: A Comparative
Analysis. New York: Praeger, 1984.

Domar, E. D. Essays in the Theory of Economic
Growth. New York: Oxford University Press, 1957.

Douglas, Roger. "The Politics of Successful
Structural Reforms." Wall Street Journal,
January 17, 1990.

Downs, Anthony. An Economic Theory of Democracy. New
York: Harper, 1957.

"Economic Reforms in the European Centrally Planned
Economies, ECE." Economic Studies, no. 1.
(1989).

EFTA Bulletin, February 1986, January 1987, and
March 1989.

"EFTA-EC Relations after the White Paper." EFTA
Bulletin, March 1987.

"EFTA-EC Relations as Observed by Swedish Trade
Unions." EFTA Bulletin, January 1988.

Ekmecic, Milorad. Stvaranje Jugoslavije 1790-1918.
[The formation of yugoslavia 1790-1918]. Belgrade:
Prosveta, 1989.

Ekonomska politika. [Socialist self-management]. no.
2005. Belgrade, 1990.

Elliot, J. E. Comparative Economic Systems.
Englewood Cliffs, N. J.: Prentice Hall, 1973.

Fabinc, Ivo. "F. I. Yugoslavia: A Newly
Industrialized European Country." In The World

Economy and the _Spatial_ _Organization_ of _Power_. Arie Schachar and Sture Oberg, eds. Avebury: Gower Publishing Company, 1990: 233-240.

____. "The Economic Rationality on the Threshold of Economic Reform." In _Problemi_ _Reforme_ _Privrednog_ _Sistema_ _SFR_ _Jugoslavije:_ _Konzorcij_ _Ekonomskih_ _Instituta_ _za_ _Makroprojekt_ _Privredni_ _Sistem_ _SFRJ._ Zagreb: Globus, 1989: 441-59.

____. "The Transition to a New Social Structure." Bellaggio, a conference, University of Maryland, March 13-15, 1990.

Federal Economic Council, 7th sess., February 17, 1989. Belgrade.

Friedman, Milton. Interview with Drago Baum in _Privredni_ _Vjesnik_, February 15, 1990.

Furubotn, Erik, and Svetozar Pejovich. "The Property Right Structure and the Behavior of the Firm in the Socialist State: The Example of Yugoslavia." _Zeitschrift_ _fur_ _Nationaloeconomie_. no. 3-4 (1970).

Gabrisch, H., and K. Laski, et al. _Transition_ _from_ _the_ _Command_ _to_ _a_ _Market_ _Economy_. W.I.I.W. (WKEN 1990): 1.

Galbraith, J. K. _Ekonomika_ _I_ _Drustveni_ _Ciljevi_ [Economic and Public Purpose]. Rijeka: Otokar Kersovani, 1976.

Goldsmith, R. _Financial_ _Structure_ _and_ _Development_. New Haven, Conn.: Yale University Press, 1969.

Goldstein, S., and M. Korosic. "Krijeme Radikalnih Promjena" ["The time of radical changes"]. _Danas_, December 1, 1987.

Grbic, Cedo. _Socijalizam_ _i_ _Rad_ _Privatnim_ _Sredstvima_ [Socialism and work with private means of production]. Zagreb: Printers and Publishers/Zagreb-Samobor, 1984.

Harrod, R. F. "An Essay in Dynamic Theory." _Economic_ _Journal_, June 1939.

Harsanyi, John. "Can the Maximum Principle Serve As A Basis for Morality"? _American_ _Political_ _Science_ _Review_, June 1975a.

____. "Nonlinear Social Welfare Functions, Theory and Decisions." _American_ _Political_ _Science_ _Review_, August 1975b.

Hebbert, Michael, and Jens Christian Hansen, eds. "Unfamiliar Territory: the Reshaping of European Geography." With Ivo Fabinc in _F._ _I._ _Yugoslavia_ _in_ _Transition_. pp. 166-70. Avebury: Gower, 1990.

Horvat, Branko. _Ekonomski_ _Modeli_ [Economic models]. Zagreb: Economics Institute, 1964.

____. _Politika_ _Ekonomija_ _Socijalizma_ [Political economy of socialism] Zagreb: Globus, 1983.

Inotai, A. "Economic Relations between the CMEA and the EC: Facts, Trends, Prospects." Acta Oeconomica (Budapest) March-April 1988.

Irvin, Zachary T. "Yugoslavia's Foreign Policy in Southeastern Europe." Problems of Balkan Security, Paul S. Shoup and George W. Hoffman, eds., pp. 166-70. Washington, D. C.: Wilson Center Press, 1990.

Johnson, Harry G., ed. Economic Nationalism in Old and New States. Chicago: University of Chicago Press, 1967.

Jovanovic, Aleksandra. "Ward-Vanek's Model and the Model of the Yugoslav Firm." Ekonomska Misao. vol. 1. (1989).

Jovanovic, M. "Podloga za Brze Razmisljane" (A basis for faster reflection). Ekonomska Politika March 14, 1988.

Korac, M. Socijalisticki Sampoupravni Nacin Proizvodnje Komunist. [Communist methods of management] vol. 1. Book 3. Belgrade, 1977.

Kornai, J. "The Hungarian Reform Process: Visions, Hopes and Reality." Journal of Economic Literature, December 1986.

Labus, Miroljub. "Evolution of the Yugoslav Firm." European University Institute. Florence, 1986.

Lenin, V. I. Izabrana Djela. [Selected works] Vol. II. Book I. Zagreb: Kultura, 1950: 107.

Lopandic, D. "EEZ, Sredozemne Zemlje i Polozaj Jugoslavije" ("EEC, mediterranean countries and the position of yugoslavia"). Medjunarodni Problemi, March 1984.

Macesich, George. "Workers' Management." Yugoslavia: Theory and Practice of Development Planning. Charlottesville: University Press of Virginia, 1964.

_____. "The Firm." Yugoslavia: Theory and Practice of Development Planning. Charlottesville: University Press of Virginia, 1964: 80-94.

_____. "The Theory of Economic Integration and the Experience of the Balkan and Danubian Countries Before 1914." Proceedings of the First International Congress on Southeast European Studies, Sofia, Bulgaria, 1966; F. S. U. Slavic Papers, vol. 1 (1967).

_____. "Economic Theory and the Austro-Hungarian Ausgleich of 1867" [Der osterreichisch-ungarische ausgleich, 1867]. Ludovit Holitik, ed. Bratislava: Slovak Academy, 1971.

_____. Geldpolitik in Einem Gemeinsamen Europaischen Markt [Money in a common-market setting]. Baden-Baden: Nomos Verlagsgesellschaft, 1972.

_____. Economic Nationalism and Stability. New York: Praeger, 1985.

_____. "Money and a Common Market: Lessons from an Early American Experience." In Problemi privrednog razvoja i privrednog sistema jugoslavije [Problems of economic development and the economic system in yugoslavia]. Dragomir Vojnic, Zvonimir Baletic, Ante Cicin-Sain, et al., eds. Zagreb: Globus, 1989.

Macesich, George, ed., with R. Lang and D. Vojnic. Essays on the Political Economy of Yugoslavia. Zagreb: Informator, 1982.

_____. R. Lang and D. Vojnic. Essays on the Yugoslav Economic Model. New York: Praeger, 1989.

Mandel, E. Rasprava O Marksistickoj Ekonomiji [Treatise on the marxist economy] vol. 2. Sarajevo: Veselin Naslesa, 1970.

Markovic, Petar, and Vladimir Stipetic, eds. Brzi Razvoj Agroindustrijskog Kompleksa-Preduslov Stabilizacije Privrednog Napretka Jugoslavije u Iducem Periodu [Faster development of the agro-industrial complex - a prerequisite for Yugoslavia's stable economic growth in the coming period]. Belgrade: Commission on the Federal Social Councils for Economic Stabilization Problems and Centar za Radnicko Samoupravljanje, 1982.

Marx, Karl. Das Kapital vol. 1. Belgrade: Kultura.

Mesarovic, M. D., and Y. Takahara. Abstract Systems Theory. Springer Verlag, 1989.

Mihajlovic, K. Ekonomska Stvarnost Jugoslavije. [The real yugoslav economy]. Belgrade, 1981.

Montias, M. The Structure of Economic Systems. New Haven, Conn.: Yale University, 1976.

Neuberger, E., and W. Duffy. Comparative Economic Systems: A Decisionmaking Approach. Boston: Allyn and Bacon, 1976.

Olson, Mancur. The Logic of Collective Action. Cambridge, Mass.: Belknap, 1971.

_____. The Rise and Decline of Nations. New Haven, Conn.: Yale University Press, 1982.

Petkovic, Ranko. Nonaligned Yugoslavia and the Contemporary World: The Foreign Policy of Yugoslavia: 1945-85. Zagreb: Mendunarodna Politika Skolska Knjiga, 1986.

Pleterski, Janko. Narodi, Jugoslavija, Revolucija. [The people, yugoslavia, revolution]. Ljubljana: Drzavna Zalozba Slovenije, 1986.

Prasnikar, Janez, and Jan Svejnar. "Workers' Participation and Management vs. Social Ownership and Government Policies: Yugoslav Lessons for

217

Transforming Socialist Economies." Department of Economics. working paper. no. 264, University of Pittsburgh, 1990.

Ranis, Gustav. "The Role of Institutions in Transition Growth: The East Asian Newly Industrializing Countries." World Development 17, no. 19. (1989).

Rawls, John. A Theory of Justice. Cambridge, Mass.: Belknap, 1971.

Roberts, Paul Craig. "An American Supply Sider in Moscow." The Wall Street Journal/Europe, June 27, 1989.

Rubinstein, Alvin Z. Yugoslavia and the Nonaligned World. Princeton, N.J.: Princeton University Press, 1970.

Sandmo, Agnar. "Buchanan on Political Economy, A Review Article." Journal of Economic Literature, March 1990, pp. 50-65.

Schachar, Arie, and Sture Oberg, eds. "The World Economy and the Spatial Organization of Power." In F. I. Yugoslavia: A Newly Industrialized European Country, edited by Ivo Fabinc, pp. 233-40. Avebury: Gower, 1990.

Sik, O. Treci Put [Der dritte weg] [The third time]. Zagreb: Globus, 1983: 173-4.

_____. Ein Wirtschaftssystem der Zukunft [An economy of the future]. Springer Verlag, 1985.

Simon, Andras. "Eastern Europe's Movement to Capitalism: Hard Landing or Soft Landing?" (Mimeographed). Link Project Meeting, New York, March 7-8, 1990, p. 1.

Sluzbeni [official laws] list SFRJ for 1988, 1989, and 1990 on financial operations, enterprises, securities, money market and capital markets; Yugoslav bank for international economic cooperation, compulsory settlement, bankruptcy, and liquidation; financial rehabilitation, bankruptcy, and liquidation of banks and other financial organizations; social capital circulation and management; federal agency for deposit insurance and bank rehabilitation; foreign investment law and foreign exchange law; social capital circulation and management; federal agency for deposit insurance and bank rehabilitation; foreign investment and foreign exchange.

Sokolovic, Dz. "Potrebe, planiranje, razvoj" [Needs, planning, development]. In Suvremeno drustvo i sociologija [The modern society and sociology], pp. 233-40. Zagreb: Globus and the Department of Sociology/Philosophy faculty of Zagreb, 1986.

Stanovnik, J. Mednarodni Gospodarski sistem

[International economic system]. Ljubljana: Drzavna Zalozba Slovenije, 1982.

Statisticki godisnjak jugoslavije [Yugoslav statistical annual] (1989): 100.

Supply-Side Economics, Theory and Results: An Assessment of the American Experience in the 1980's. Washington, D.C.: Institute for Political Economy, January 1989.

Stajner, Rikard. "Contemporary Developments in Western Europe: The Position and Role in International Relations and Interests of Yugoslavia." Belgrade: Center for Strategic Studies, 1986.

Szamuely, L. "Prospects of Economic Reform in the European CMEA Countries." Acta Oeconomica 36, nos. 1-2: 56-65.

Vanek, Jaroslav. The General Theory of Labor-Managed Market Economy. Ithaca, NY: Cornell University Press, 1970.

Vojnic, Dragomir. Ekonomska Stabilizacija i Ekonomska Kriza [Economic stabilization and economic crisis]. Zagreb: Economics Institute and Globus, 1986.

_____. "Problems from Technological Lag and Structural Adjustment to Institutional Changes." In Strukturno Prilagodjavanje Privred sr Hrvatske Uvjetima Stabilizacije [Structural adjustment of the croatian economy to conditions of stabilization]. Zagreb: Informator, 1988.

_____. Current Problems of Economic Flows and Economic Policy in Yugoslavia. Zagreb: Economics Institute, 1988.

_____. "The Socioeconomic Model of Self-Management in Essays on the Yugoslav Economic Model. George Macesich, ed., with Rikard Lang and Dragomir Vojnic. New York: Praeger, 1989.

Vranicki, P. Samoupravljanje Kao Permanentna Revolucija. [Self-management as the absolute revolution]. Zagreb: CKD, 1985.

Vukadinovic, Radovan. "Yugoslavia's Foreign Policy in the Period Ahead." Review of International Affairs 38, no. 901 (Belgrade 1987): 13-4.

Vukadinovic, Radovan, and Vlatko Mileta. Evropa Iza Ugla [Europe behind the corner]. Zagreb: August Cesarec, 1990.

Ziberna, M. "Economic Relations between Yugoslavia and the European Economic Community." Yugoslav Survey, January 1987.

Zic, Z. "Savremena Kretanja u Zapadnoj Evropi-Polozaj i Uloga u Medjunarodnim Odnosima" [Contemporary developments in western europe-the

position and role in international relations]
Pregled 2 (1987).

Zimmermann, Warren. "U.S.A. and Yugoslavia."
<u>Review of International Affairs</u> 16, no. 960
(Belgrade 1990): 6-8.

Index

decentralization of,
68, 71; partici-
pation in, 71-72,
128; Socialist,
147-49; working
class and, 154;
Yugoslav govern-
ment and, 59, 88
Delors, Jacques, 179
Democracy: European in-
dustrial, 107-8; poli-
tical, 7, 129-30;
self-management, 120,
121. See also
Self-management system
Deregulation, in
Markovic government,
56
Development Fund, 171
Discrimination, 8
Dobb, Maurice H., 151-
52
Downs, Anthony, 4-5, 7
Duffy, W., 147

Eastern Europe: col-
lapse of socialist
system in, 127;
effect of opening
of, 111, 112
Economic growth rate,
24-25, 45
Economic insti-
tutions. See
Business insti-
tutions
Economic nationalism:
appeal of, 9; ex-
planation of, 9-
10; implications
of, 408
Economic reform:
capital imports
and, 204-8; ex-
planation and types
of, 43; failures of,
135-37; goals for,
163-64; in Markovic
government, 55-57;
of mid-1970s, 46-47;
of 1965, 46; of

1990s, 48-52; princi-
ples for, 68-69, 139,
142-43, 208-10; re-
sults of, 201
Economics: insti-
tutional, 44, tran-
sitional, 39.
See also Supply-
side economics
Economics Institute
(Zagreb), 18
Economic stabili-
zation program, 18-19
Economic system: ex-
planation and com-
ponents of, 41-42;
macroeconomic ad-
justment vs. changes
in, 57-59; make up
of Yugoslavia, 40;
transition problems
of, 44-48; See also
Transition problems
Economy: effect of
central planning
system on, 122; post-
World War II tran-
sition to command,
45-46; problems of
Yugoslav, 19-20, 165-
66. See also
Agreement economy;
Market economy
Education. See
Business education
programs
Enterprise Law, 169-71
EUREKA project, 177-78
Europe: ability to
reach out to, 193-99;
economics and future
of, 176-78; ideal
for, 97-98; inte-
gration with, 94-95,
175-84, 202-4; move
of capital to, 211-
12; reapproachment
with, 190, 195
European Bank, 210
European Community (EC):
evolution of, 95;

problems in, 104-5;
work ethic in, 110

World Bank, 183
World War I, 175
World War II, 175,
203

Yugoslavia: compara-
tive advantage of,
208-10; directions
for, 11; economic
crisis of 1970s
and 1980s in, 17-
18; economic
profile of, 17;
and European inte-
gration, 178-80,
182-84; federal
system in, 87; as
federation, 125,
138, 190-91, 199;
foreign aid for,
210; leadership
in, 4; liberation
of, 119-20; multi-
national character
of, 44-45, 122, 196,
203; multi-party
system for, 181-82,
189; overview of,
1-2; position in non-
aligned movement, 180-
82, 187; relationship
with Europe, 175-78;
social processes of
1970s in, 31-32;
tourism in, 175;
Western aid for re-
form in, 210-12
Yugoslav government:
changes in, 49;
decisionmaking by,
59, 88; economic
intervention by, 83,
124, 137; interaction
with Europe set up by,
94
Yugoslav republics: con-
flict within, 138, 139;
decisionmaking by, 71-

72; effect of eco-
nomic intervention
on, 124- 25; sharing
in dialogue by, 91-
92; transition to
community of, 92,
98-99; unrest in,
203-4. See also
individual re-
publics

229

About the Editors and Contributors

LJUBISA S. ADAMOVIC graduated with a degree in economics from the University of Belgrade. He is chairman of the department of international economics, University of Belgrade. He has served as a senior research fellow and research economist for the Institute of International Politics and Economics (Belgrade), a commentator on international economic affairs for the Yugoslav National Telecast System, and special advisor to the Federal Secretariat for Foreign Affairs of Yugoslavia. He is the author of many books and articles on foreign trade, international trade and finance, trade theory, international marketing, multinational business, economic research, and journalism. He is a visiting professor and research scholar at the Center for Yugoslav-American Studies, Research, and Exchanges at Florida State University and a member of the Joint Yugoslav-American Advisory Council and Academic Committee for the Center for Yugoslav-American Studies, Research, and Exchanges.

STOJAN BULAT graduated from the University of Belgrade with a Ph.D. in political science. He received his master's degree in economics from Florida State University. At the University of Belgrade, he was associate dean of the Faculty of Political Science, executive secretary of the Center for International Studies, and president of the Labor Committee, City Council of Belgrade. He is a member of the Board of Editors and president of the Yugoslav Center for Publications in Economics and a member of the Academic Council in the Yugoslav Institute for Journalism. His books, papers, and articles deal with production, management, self-management, money, inflation and stabilization. He is a visiting scholar at the Center for Yugoslav-American Studies, Research, and Exchanges at Florida State University.

MARSHALL R. COLBERG graduated from the University of Michigan with a Ph.D. in economics. He has taught at the University of Michigan, the University of Virginia, the Florida State University London program, and the University of Belgrade. He served as president of the Southern Economic Association and on the Economic Education Committee of the American Economic Association. He has written books and articles on business economics, price theory, human capital, wartime production controls, social security, labor law, taxation, and the Yugoslav economy. He is associate director of the Center for Yugoslav-American Studies, Research, and Exchanges at Florida State University.

DIMITRIJE DIMITRIJEVIC graduated from the Faculty of Law, University of Belgrade, and received his Ph.D. in economics from the University of Zagreb. He also studied in the United States under a Ford Foundation scholarship and was a visiting professor at the University of Chicago. He is currently professor of economics, Faculty of Political Sciences, University of Skopje. He is the retired general manager of the National Bank of Yugoslavia (the central bank) and the author of numerous books and articles on monetary analysis, money and finance, money supply process, and commercial banking. He is presently a visiting professor of economics at Florida State University through the Center for Yugoslav-American Studies, Research, and Exchanges.

IVO FABINC graduated from the University of Belgrade with a Ph.D. in economics. He has served as Rector of the University of Ljubljana; as dean of the Faculty of Economics, University of Ljubljana; as assistant director of the Institute for Foreign Trade in Belgrade; and as chairman of the Federal Committee for Foreign Trade in Belgrade. He has written numerous articles and monographs on international economic relations, economic policy (macroeconomics), and federalism.

232

ALEKSANDRA JOVANOVIC graduated in law from the University of Belgrade and holds a master's degree in economics from the same university. She is a research and teaching assistant in the department of economics at the Faculty of Law, University of Belgrade. Her research focuses on the influence of institutional arrangements on economic efficiency. She is working on her Ph.D. and is a research associate at the Center for Yugoslav-American Studies, Research, and Exchanges at Florida State University.

RIKARD LANG graduated with an LL.D. from the University of Zagreb. He served as professor of political economy at the University of Zagreb (1947-83); and as professor of postgraduate studies at Zagreb and other universities. He is the former director of the Zagreb Economics Institute 1954-74 and is presently serving as its research advisor. He was a Ford Rotating Research Professor at the University of California, Berkeley (1964-65). He is a former member of the UN Economic, Employment, and Development Commission and served as a UN expert in various countries and as a consultant to many international organizations. He has published widely on the political economy under conditions of socialist self-management, on the theory of economic development, on international economic relations, on the theory of economic systems, and on reform.

GEORGE MACESICH received his Ph.D. from the University of Chicago in economics and did his undergraduate work at George Washington University. He is the founding director of the Center for Yugoslav-American Studies, Research, and Exchanges at Florida State University and professor of economics. He is an editorial consultant for several domestic and foreign professional journals, founding editor of the FSU Proceedings and Reports, and the author of over 100 articles and thirty books.

LJUBISAV MARKOVIC received his Ph.D. in economics from the University of Belgrade. He is the author of numerous books and articles relating to political economy and economic policy. He has been a member of the Yugoslav Federal Parliament, a member of the Federal Government, chairman of the Committee for Social Planning and Development Policy in the

Assembly of Yugoslavia, a member of the presidency of the Federal Conference of the Socialist Alliance, chairman of the Division of Agricultural Development in the Socialist Alliance of Yugoslavia, an elected member of the Federation Council, and a member of the president's cabinet.

ZIVKO PREGL graduated from the Faculty of Economics, the University of Ljubljana. He is a professional economist and a former Director General of the Institute for Social Planning of the SR of Slovenia. He served as Undersecretary in the Federal Executive Council of the SFR of Yugoslavia and the Director of the Federal Bureau for Prices. He has published numerous articles in specialized and scientific journals on economic, urban, and social planning, structural adjustment policy, economic conjuncture, market economic systems, and reform. He participated in seminars organized by the Alliance of Economists of Yugoslavia, UNIDO, and IBRD. He has been a guest lecturer of the Japanese and American governments. He has served as Vice-President of the Federal Executive Council of the SFR of Yugoslavia in charge of the economic and political system. He is now Deputy Prime Minister of Yugoslavia.

DUSKO SEKULIC received his Ph.D. in sociology from the University of Zagreb where he is professor of sociology. At the University of Zagreb, he has served as chairman of the sociology department, assistant dean and director of the School of Social and Humanistic Sciences, and president of the University Assembly. He was also a member of the governing board of the Research Council of the International Sociological Association. He has published in Yugoslavia and abroad in economic sociology, social stratification and research methods, marketing, planning, and self-management. He is the principal investigator on the international project Comparative Social Structure and Dynamics financed by the National Science Foundation. For 1991-92 he was a Fulbright scholar in Yugoslav and East European Studies at George Mason University, in in Fairfax, Virginia.

BERNARD SLIGER graduated with a Ph.D. in economics from Michigan State University. He has taught economics at Florida State University, Michigan State

University, Louisiana State University, and Southern University. He has served as a consultant to private and public commissions and organizations in Florida and Louisiana, as a member of the Board of Directors of the Federal Reserve Bank of Atlanta, and as a member and chairman of the American College Testing Board of Trustees. He has held memberships in the Southeastern Universities Research Association, the Universities Research Association-Executive Committee and Board of Trustees, National Association of State Universities and Land Grant Colleges, American Council on Education, ACE Labor/Higher Education Council, International Association of University Presidents, Council on Competitiveness, and the Joint Council on Economic Education Board of Trustees.

E. RAY SOLOMON graduated from the University of Wisconsin with a Ph.D. in business. He was dean of the college of business and is the Payne H. Midyette, Sr., and Charlotte Hodges Midyette Eminent Scholar Professor of Insurance at Florida State University. His published books and articles focus on risk management, employee benefits plans, life and health insurance, the economics of insurance, business ethics, and business education accreditation. He is involved in the Consortium for International Management Studies at Florida State University.

RIKARD STAJNER studied economics at the University of Zagreb and obtained his Ph.D. from the same university. His publications include books and scientific/professional works on economic development. He has worked as a research advisor at the Economics Institute-Zagreb and as a professor at the University of Zagreb, Faculty of Economics. He has been a member of the Executive Council of the Socialist Republic of Croatia and the Federal Executive Council and has served as the Yugoslav ambassador to Belgium and Luxembourg.

DAN VOICH, JR. received his Ph.D. in business from the University of Illinois. He is a professor of management and associate dean of the College of Business at Florida State University. He has written numerous books and articles on systems theory and analysis, organization and management theory, comparative systems, and policy formulation and decisionmaking. He participates in the activities of the Center for Yugoslav-American Studies, Research, and Exchanges at Florida State University, the University of Belgrade, and the University of Zagreb, and is involved in the Consortium for International Management Studies at Florida State University.

DRAGOMIR VOJNIC graduated with a Ph.D. in economics from the University of Zagreb, where he taught. He was one of the founders of the Zagreb Economics Institute (Ekonomski Institut) and served as its director for many years. He has published widely on the problems of economic development, the socialist self-management economic system, and reform. He has served as author and editor of the "red books," a series on Yugoslavia's economic trends and economic policies, and is the chief editor of Ekonomski Pregled. He is the chairman of the Joint Yugoslav-American Advisory Council and Academic Committee of the Center for Yugoslav-American Studies, Research, and Exchanges, at Florida State University in the United States.

ANTON VRATUSA received his Ph.D. in political science from the University of Ljubljana. He has served as director of the Institute of Social Sciences (Belgrade); and as president of the Council of the International Center for Public Enterprises in Developing Countries (Ljubljana), and has been honorary president of the Council of the International Center for Public Enterprises in Developing Countries (Ljubljana) since 1984. He is a member of the Academy of Sciences and Arts (Ljubljana) and professor of political science at the University of Belgrade and Ljubljana. He has served as vice prime minister and as deputy foreign minister of Yugoslavia. He has also served as prime minister of Slovenia; president of the Federal Chamber, Assembly of the Socialist Federal Republic of Yugoslavia (SFRY); and of the Foreign Relations Committee, Assembly of the SFRY; member of the Council of Federation; and member of numerous delegations to the United Nations. He is the author of studies on self-management and the political system in Yugoslavia and on contemporary international policy, from non-alignment to problems in international cooperation, development and peace and security.

RADOVAN VUKADINOVIC received his Ph.D. from the University of Zagreb. He is professor of international relations in the Faculty of Political Sciences of the University of Zagreb and director of the postgraduate course in international relations. He was a senior fellow in the School of International Affairs at Columbia University; editor-in-chief of the Yugoslav journal for political sciences, Politicka Misao; and dean of the Faculty of Political Sciences. He has written numerous books on international politics and is a frequent contributor to journals in Yugoslavia and abroad on international politics. He is a member of the academic committee of the Institute for East-West Security Studies in New York. He is also visiting professor and research scholar in political science at Florida State University and at the Center for Yugoslav-American Studies, Research, and Exchanges at Florida State University.